Teaching for Tomorrow

My Adventures Teaching English in Vietnam,
1998 - 2004

Hayden Sewall

© 2016, Peace Bird Publishers. Self Published Work by Hayden Sewall.
Teaching For Tomorrow: My Adventures Teaching in Vietnam, 1998-2004.

ISBN: 978-0-9984323-0-4

This book uses the typeface "Droid Serif," in both English and Vietnamese with headings in "Future Std." Some names and details have been changed, though most remain unchanged in this edition.

To Everyone Who Made This Possible

Table of Contents

Introduction 2

The First Day I was Late, the Second Day I Left Early, The Third Day I Played Hooky 5

What Doesn't Fail You Makes You Smarter 17

Teacher, We're Camping! 27

Calling Class 911 37

Cat Ba On a Shoestring 51

Toshiba, Inc. 61

Jingle (Mission) Bells 71

The Language Centre 81

We are Millionaires Already 93

Back Home 103

Introduction

Fresh out of John Brown University in Siloam Springs, Arkansas, with a graphic arts degree on my diploma, I entered the world of advertising. But even working in a best-case-scenario agency doing bank ads, mid-afternoon I would find my mind drifting back to some adventures I had had growing up—imagined ones, as a fan of Indiana Jones, and actual ones, like the trips over the border, to Mexico and Guatemala, that had developed an intrigue in me over people who had such different lives. Spending time with international friendship partners like my friend Kei from Japan, or An from Vietnam put a spark in me that never went out.

The logical conclusion in my mind was to explore my options for a job that would take me to one of these enchanting places I could call home for a while. Long story short, from 1998 to 2004, an opportunity to teach English at Vietnam Maritime University in Haiphong, Vietnam was my next career step. There I was able to practice the culture instead of just observe it. I came to cry for the tragedies of the past and celebrate the promises of the future. When I started teaching, I was surprised to find that students needed English to work in the local economy, but they also craved it to learn songs and culture. For my part, I longed for a chance to understand the intertwined history between our two countries and what makes them dream. It was a wonderful exchange.

Now, almost twenty years later, after following other calls to Phnom Penh, Cambodia, and Abu Dhabi, UAE, I am preparing to teach again elsewhere. Before going, I wanted to close the book on this wonderful chapter in my life. I have written 100 stories and essays which I hope capture the essence of teaching in a foreign land. Ten of these are included here. I hope you will enjoy reading them and share the mystique I hold in my heart for these people.

This is a collection of memories from daily spending time with my students and much of it is light-hearted. I would not be completely true to my readers or myself if I did not express that an underlying *euangelion*--a positive message--is inherent in my approach to these friendships.

While there is much to be enjoyed in a cultural exchange for both sides, there is also a strictly human urgency to aid those seeking divine encouragement. This may differ for different travelers, but this is seen for me *as a Christian* in 2 Corinthians 5:14-20 of the Bible. This may happen through my presence or a healing word, leading to the hope of a better future together in one specific family--God's family.

For those of you who have been a part of making these experiences possible, I deeply appreciate it, and I hope that you will continue on this journey with me. Has it been a good investment? Continued communication with some of my students there assure me that their lives have been charted on a better course because of it and it was indeed time well spent.

Hayden

The First Day I was Late,
the Second Day I Left Early,
the Third Day I Played Hooky.

I never thought of myself as much of a teacher. In fact, when the idea of this whole adventure, I balked initially. And if it weren't for the desires driving me to see the world—this world—I might have backed away. I'm glad I didn't. Teaching English to these young men and women has been a profound joy, but it wasn't always so. I'm thinking particularly about the first day I ever tried it.

My first morning of teaching went from nervous, to frightful, to panicky. I'll explain. I thought I knew exactly where room 121 was, but when I strutted after parking my bicycle and taking the little number ticket— my makeshift teacher bag, a few props and the pink covered navigation book in hand—I found the room I had located the previous day, empty. Puzzled, I looked around at some of the other numbers and rooms. They had students and various teachers who were preparing their books and writing on their blackboards.

"Well, this is just great," I thought. "They are going to fire me and send me home on my first day!" Not knowing much Vietnamese at all—well, ok, not knowing *any* Vietnamese—it was soon clear that my charades "lesson plan B" that I was saving in case that students didn't know English—well, that was needed now. I went back to the administration building and conceded defeat, basically telling them that my class had already started and I was foolishly and hopelessly lost. Before I ran into anyone important though, an off-duty teacher saw me looking confused and said, basically, "come on and go with me." He procured his motorcycle, and even though I didn't have a helmet (a "no-no" for us, but not for the Vietnamese at that time) I obeyed out of urgency, and we hopped onto Lach Tray street where he drove like a banshee, about a third of a mile. There, was another gate. Another world. "I went rummaging through my teacher manpurse trying to find some change, to which he said no, no, no, and I thankfully darted off, hoping somebody was still around.

It didn't take too long to find the other room 121. When I came, a rustling of young bustling men in the room suddenly subsided and instead I found an army of rigid young warriors standing at attention. I had been told, by a former teacher actually, that this is how we did it, and so I knew at this moment what to do. I walked across the room and firmly laid my stuff on the table and smiled stoically; waving my hand so everyone could sit down. Ten minutes late. Not fired. '*We cool.*' Hello. Deep breath. Now what?

The only thing I knew to break the awkwardness was to find the chalk. Looking around, I didn't see any. Suddenly a kid burst up out of his seat and shuffled up to the front. He threw some chalk on the table and a notebook with the students' names, and sat down quickly.

"Ah! good," I thought. Let's call roll.

So I grabbed the chalk, wrote my name. All the students dutifully tried to say my name. There was a rustling of people getting their notebooks out. And then, I said, "Let's see who is here." *Gosh, this was awkward.* So I start reading the names. "Le Kwee,...Bon?"—turns out, the uncertainty of my pronunciation caused me to say it with the proper tone and a kid shot up his hand and said "Caw!"

The next two or three brought momentary stare followed by some people pointing at who they thought I was saying, and the kid would give me a kind of hesitary "caw?" After a few of these, I got wise and said, "Hey, can you read the rest of 'em, while I write some stuff on the board?" Maybe it was just me, but the kid was like, "I thought you'd never ask."

The way our schedule was laid out, we didn't teach every day, and the first day had been near the end of the week, so the second day of teaching trailed a slow and lazy weekend, which gave us all a great time of better informed preparation for the coming first full-week of teaching. In my mind, I was going to please these watching walls without stepping outside the bounds of my new employers' idea of good teaching. Being a creative person and seeing how conformed and rigid everything was, I still was not sure how I was going to bridge the old and the new. What is more, I had a bit of a misunderstanding that caused the class to leave too early on the second day. The learning curve was much greater through another language, and the absence of orientation for us was partly due to the fact that we had all entered the scene late. The students themselves had certainly been briefed to make sure I taught "only English," but very little else. They also must have had noticed that I would come prepared with a wide array of Western culture. That made our school administration nervous in Communist North Vietnam.

"Teacher, can you teach us the words of *My Heart Will Go On?*"

"Teach you the words? In English? I'm not sure where I'm going to find them." Those days were on the verge of the internet age, but not to worry, the song itself was emblazoned on almost everybody's school binder.

"I see that you have it. Here, let me borrow it and I'll write it up on the board then." As we launched into the song, all the boys (yes, it is all boys) went into this sort of trance and started swaying back and forth like we were singing Michael Jackson's "We Are the World" (This is another song they love). They all began singing with this mesmerized drunk swagger *"Every time in my dreams, I see you, I feeeeeeel you..."*

Suddenly, I felt disgusted. This is not teaching English! But they were all lost in it, so we I just went along with it.

"Teacher can we sing '*Nothing's Gonna Change My Love For You?*"

"No!!"... "I mean, absolutely not. We are going to learn shipmanship. Not that Titanic isn't completely irrelevant at a Maritime University. Let's read from your book. We opened the little pink book of text-only called *English For Seafarers* and I started reading, "Vessels used for the transportation of cargo and passengers: general cargo ships, dry bulk carriers, liquid bulk carriers, container ships,"

"Teacher! Slower, *Slower*!!"

"Yes, you're right. Let's repeat them. I will say them slowly... Ro/Ro ships (Lolo sheeps), coasters (costers), reefers (rrweefers), Lash-vessels (wash wessels), heavy-load vessels, timber carriers, multipurpose vessels and passenger ships. I know what. Let me ask you all a question based on what you just heard read. What is a large sized boat that travels across the sea?"

Blank stares. I was just testing them out and even used hand motions, but it was clear enough that basic English was going to be needed here.

"Teacher, I have a question, what is the difference between a lightship and a tug?" This came from a smart kid on the front row.

Well, it was also clear enough too that we were on different levels entirely in this same basic class. I suddenly wanted to ask him how he spoke perfectly. I was also disturbed because it seemed that fewer people were coming in with each period. I had definitely lost a handful of zero-English speakers.

"Hey guys, how about I call roll and we'll get out early." We were supposed to do this first and last period to make them all come back. The crowd got happy, but "can I do this?" Yikes, well it's done, so let's roll with it.

I tried calling role a little extra slow. "Le Quy Bon. Le Quyyy Bon."

"He's Chewin."

"I'm sorry?"

"He's Chewin," somebody else said.

"Le Ngoc Thanh."

"Chewin."

"What does that *mean*???... Nguyen Van Thai."

"Caw." I just assumed at this point that Chewin meant something in Vietnamese, but later somebody explained it to me. They were saying "truant," which means skipping school – due to my Southern roots, I'd only known the phrase 'hooky.' So much for teaching English, my students knew more words than I did, and they knew all the British words too.

"Ok, let's just call it a day, while I try to think of some fillers on Wednesday." But there wasn't a Wednesday. The students came up with a filler of their own that swallowed up the whole day whole.

So, the whole thing really started after that evening, but it may have been set in motion the moment I let them out. As the students all poured into the bicycle room early, I ducked out, hoping that no one important would put two-and-two together that I'd let them out five minutes before everybody else. The bicycle keeper, himself just a kid, didn't care, but somebody might. When I emerged at the front gate, the students were all pouring out. There was this handsome tall kid, I had noticed him because he was the student in the class who had been elected to be the assistant— they called it a monitor—so he was kind of a leader, and had been present both times. I pulled him off—he may have thought he was in trouble. I said, "I need to buy a shirt. Soccer shirt, maybe. Can you help me?"

Of course I knew how to buy a shirt. I wanted an excuse to try and get to know this guy outside class because I thought, as the monitor, he might be able to also become a good cultural informant. He didn't have the best English, but it was above average—mostly I think they picked him because he was cool. He was much obliged, and changed his plans immediately. From then on, Khanh became my best friend. He was so good to me, taking me to buy the shirt and then meet his parents and everything. I was going to have to work now not to show him favoritism. But being there to change hearts and souls, I didn't think I was going to do it by repeating the words " *buoyage vessels,... survey vessels,... supply boats, ...SAR-vessels,...and so on.*" So Khanh and I hung out a bit on Tuesday too, when his other classes were done.

Before the evening of that second class, another kid in the class named Vinh came over. He had a great sophisticated way about him something about him felt very proper—I thought the he was probably a poster-child for the kind of revolutionary conformist that the new government was trying to create, obviously another model looked up to by his peers and we talked for hours about his view of the world. I can't remember what we talked about, but it must have fed that impression of him, whatever it was. I left feeling that he would be a good student in class. Nothing more, really. I think breaking the ice with both of these guys gave them a bit of felt license to show off their new teacher, so on the morning of class, I got dressed up in a fancy shirt and trousers and prepared the lesson plan. I was proud of myself this time, having dug up several games given to us in our training that I was ready to try out. No more letting people out early. But as I was thinking about leaving the apartment, Vinh showed up at the door. He said "Are you ready?"

I said "Oh? ...Ok. You want to take me? That's fine." I thought he wanted to chauffer me to class on his Honda Supercub. He gave me some flowers, and this may have been the first moment I realize that boys did that here, so I awkwardly went rummaging for something to put them in, and thought that might be the strangest thing that happened today.

"Can you ride on the back of this motorbike? We're going to festival today."

"*Festival*? I...um. What?... I need to teach. ...No! I would have to cancel class, to um...what festival are we going to?" I obviously wanted to say 'yes' to something as interesting as a festival.

"Don't worry teacher. I already took care of that. Are you ready?"

At first I thought maybe he wasn't for real, but yes, we glided on by the gate where tons of other kids were pouring into their classes. *I am going to die for this,* I thought. I sure hoped it was going to be worth it. "Where is this festival?"

"Dosun. It's my hometown, teacher!"

"Dosun??? The well-known beach was a half-hour ride out of town. So there we were, playing chewin. The teacher. I closed my eyes and painfully imagined Khanh, as monitor, having to manage the unruly class because he had no idea where the teacher went. "Are you sure class is cancelled?"

As if to answer, Khanh came humming up behind us on his scooter.

Oh great, it's a conspiracy.

"Don't worry teacher, Chinh and Duc are coming too, and then we'll have lunch at my house."

Bleak, salty air filled the flat landscape of Dosun. As we cut through it like a butter knife, I wondered what "The Boys of Summer" by Don Henley sounded like to a Vietnamese. We were obviously in a hurry, as Vinh didn't say too much, and Khanh had veered off now to fetch the other boys as promised. As we approached, the traffic on the straight ribbon road grew thick and our bodies brushed up against other festivalgoers squeezing by. The sting of unprofessionalism in this case hadn't left me. I started to wonder what Ferris Bueller might have done as a teacher.

"We're here, teacher!" We had veered off course to apparently his house – a "tiny house" – elegant, simple square beauty all by itself on sandy property that felt like the frontier. Soup was on, and the little home was abuzz with the excitement of the big day. 'Mom' sacrificially sat by the hearth to make sure the rest of us would have a good day, and we were met by the three others and a couple more from my class. "Đừng quên mũ mà. Trời nắng em quí"

Vinh dove into a closet and pulled out hats for us. Mine looked like something out of a Monet painting, garnered with bouquets of roses. Another different kid named Vinh who I haven't mentioned yet must have seen the sour look on my face, and so he rapidly switched his with mine – a plain one. All of us were going out in ladies' hats.

We walked along the terrace, through a couple of rice fields and smack into a crowd of people. The smells of hot caramel snacks and freshly cut sugarcane fought against the familiar state-fair mix of crushed hay and animal feces mixed with the bodies of a thousand spectators. By this time, I understood that we were going to the Dosun Buffalo fighting festival, held annually in mid-September. We seemed to have already found ourselves in one of the parades, as a big water buffalo moo'ed an obvious 'coming through' and several guys in shimmery red and bright yellow costumes acted as though I were not unusual. I had my big Canon Rebel film camera, and I shot some pictures—a man with a Vietnamese conical hat was carrying some sort of float—a decoration I might have later known was dedicated to the goddess of the sea. He gave me a smile. My escorts were very protective, telling me several times to watch my wallet. This would have been easy to lose because I was so immersed in the scene.

Finally, we came up against the stone-stepped seating arena, which I'm sure sees more guests on this day than the rest of the year. It was standing room only—we were not getting a seat, even here in the cheap seats. Across from us was more of a proper stadium, which was mostly full of more uppity cadres and better-dressed dignitaries. Our timing was such that the Buffalos were already charging, a good distance, mind you, and it was hard to make out the whole process. The buffalos were clearly marked by big painted numbers on their sides. Apparently, two or four men would hover by the agitated beast with wooden restraining poles, as he was supposed to feel free to let his anxiety out on the opposing buffalo once the poles were released—I thought that if I were a buffalo, that target might be the least on my mind.

Sometimes, when these pulled back, the buffalo just kind of sat there as if to ponder this odd kind of anti-sport—other times they would dutifully charge the other buffalo, as if trained. The sport struck me as being a little strange too, because the buffalos collided and then just sat there with their horns locked. The first one to turn and run like a baby would disqualify a whole village. The winner of the whole thing would be killed for his services and offered to the goddess while his village became the talk of the town for a whole year. It was a worthy sacrifice, I suppose, but if someone had told me, I might have run back to class and taught English dutifully like a good buffalo.

The sheer raw energy of locked horns made the battlefield strangely motionless at times, as though admiring a sculpture of strength and virility, but the potential energy caught between locked horns was reflected in the cheers and jeers of an exhilarated crowd. The longer each pair of titans sat there locked in angst, the louder it roared. No doubt there was money involved.

One of the losers ran right at us. We were near a concession stand, and I don't think the concessioners had been properly trained to handle a runaway buffalo. They just kind of vacillated on whether to throw their arms around their precious popcorn stash or high-tail it the other way. Never mind, the whole thing was neutralized by a buffalo patrol that showed up in the nick of time. Crowds weren't always cheering at the proper times, and I was irked because I thought the buffalo charging at us was about the craziest thing I'd ever seen.

We stayed long. Granted—buffalos are a lot more interesting than school assembly speeches. The sqwaky commentator became a constant blur of noise to me, and the crowd didn't diminish, though we did manage to finally find a place to rest our haunches. As the fumes of sun-baked grass and sweat fused with the noonday heat, we all began to wish for shade and air, or else one of the umbrellas dotting the crowds. My ladies' hat made a pretty good fan. The toothless villagers all around us spoke in a distinctly different tone that reminded me of rednecks where I came from. (I imagined them all saying 'the south shall rise again,' but quickly silenced that inappropriate thought.) As it were, despite the thrill of seeing another buffalo, there was a lot of time between duels to think in English so I chose to think about what I was going to tell Brian and Manny when we reviewed our lesson-planning notes tonight. I wondered if this might not be a better classroom.

"Would you like to speak English?" I asked to one of the boys. He just stared blankly for a second, and then turned to his friend with a barrage of inquisitive Vietnamese. "Yes teacher, he wants," offered a helpful friend.

As the time broiled on, our expectations heightened, for the quality had certainly improved. Number forty-two and seventeen stared off, as we all imagined the impact of being hit by a truck. In this case, no. They just loitered there in front of everyone, for two full minutes grunting thunder but showing none. Seventeen takes a nip at forty-two's ear—and the anxious crowd goes suddenly wild. There's a lot of heavy eating in store too—the buffalos giving it their all and by this time smashing. Smashing. Smashing. Locked horns. Seventeen isn't giving up, though it's taken a gash to his flank. I don't know how forty-two rolled back up on his toes so quickly. Seventeen backs down and meanders off, anticlimactically. A minute and a half goes by. It's not over until the hooves cross the hilt. But no, he charged! The announcer is *ca-la-la-la-la-la* on the PA, the crowds are shrill. Seventeen manages to clip forty-two on the haunch. His nemesis is really angry now, more shamed than hurt. They lock horns a second time. This will determine it. People in the cheap seats are standing now. I hear someone shout at it like it's his own kid. Wow look, forty-two looks done!

Convinced he's not to win, he dives to the loser's corner, unaware that this is the winners' bracket. There's no towel to throw. Seventeen senses the cue and corners forty-two to the doom. The buffalo squad knows he's down, but how do you quench such flames? Nobody wants to eat punctured meat. Twirling Buddhist flags and poking both creatures with sticks does nothing. This one may need time. The crowd is beyond satisfied.

We finished with a filling meal and soccer on the beach. How can I say anything ill about Vietnam in this moment? My camera is full, my mouth simmering with the taste of shrimp spring rolls and overflowing with thanks for 'mom,' who's kept the hearth throughout the day. The boys had plenty to say about the day, and I suppose their district's buffalo lost his game—there's only one winner, but when I heard the prize was a thousand dollars, I joined in on a silent moment of regret. But nothing put a damper on our day. I came home with a tan and whether or not I'd get a tanning didn't seem to matter anymore. It had indeed been worth it all—for the first time, I'd enjoyed something purely Vietnamese.

The funniest thing is, I never heard another word about it. No pink slip of any kind, or direct inquiry into my strange way of teaching *in abstentia*. I guess this culture just has laid-back qualities. But one certain strain of penance has since fallen on me—delivered to my bedside, inflicted by the gods. For ever since that day, now seventeen years old, I've had this reoccurring dream of students, sitting around waiting. Wondering if I'm ever going to show up teaching.

What Doesn't Fail You Makes You Smarter

Spending time with friends on weekends (and class time) was one thing, but come exam time, Brian and Manny and I began making plans for all-out war against the students. Manny's tests were, well, shall we say—*effective?* Our supervisor Mrs. Thanh one meeting simply gave us a perplexed look after trying to take one. "They look very simple indeed, but when you try to take them, you can't answer even one!" We began imitating Manny's style by making simple matching tests—for one thing, they were easy to grade—but the tests did have one fatal weakness. They were simple number codes: A, D, C, A, A, B, etc, which meant that the tests became less about the information and more about how the students could collaborate to crack the code. In other words, Manny was perhaps unwittingly setting up the students to actually use their brains in an unlikely way. The real test was not the English language of Seafarers, but the ancient Art of War with which the Vietnamese have had a lot of experience.

Mao Tse Tung would be pleased. *"We should always use our brains and think everything over carefully. A common saying goes, 'Knit your brows and you will hit upon a stratagem.' In other words much thinking yields wisdom. In order to get rid of the blindness that exists to a serious extent in our Party, we must encourage our comrades to think, to learn the method of analysis and to cultivate the habit of analysis."*[1]. We marveled at the students ingenuity and had to give them credit. After all, learning a few pages in the book to ace the test might have taken a couple of days—it was obvious the students had been as tuned-in to the ways of war as General Manny was in the field. They had to have spent weeks mastering their tactics, weaving together the most elaborate plans to insure that no student got left behind.

Taking our cues from the writings of Sun Tzu, who is credited with the great military classic *The Art of War* so often quoted by Ho Chi Minh and Vo Nguyen Giap, we were determined to fight for the American ideals of honesty and integrity and fairness against the students' obvious value of helping their peers or saving face when a test seemed to be just too hard.

Another thing that blew all of our minds was that at the end of the day, all the students were moved up to the next level whether they had performed well or not. This was due to the Communist value of keeping cells together for life.

"If that is the case, why all this cheating?" My only theory on the matter still stands. It has never been about the grade—cheating and games are two things that are simply fun in their own right. Not only was it fun, but it was a chance for the students to express their love for one another in the face of adversity, taking from a quote from Uncle Ho, "Remember, the storm is a good opportunity for the pine and the cypress to show their strength and their stability." If our class had been taught by Ho Chi Minh, he might have applauded our wargames, as the art of war might take one farther than simply teaching "English for Seafarers."

The book "The Art of War" is only *attributed* to Sun Tzu, but no one is sure who wrote it. The historical figure lived and fought two hundred years before Qin Huang Di who unified China, and these words were presumably written 512 years before Jesus wrote about the art of peace. Serving king Helü of Wu just prior to what is called appropriately "the warring states period," Sun Tzu wrote the book to preserve his genius for future generations like ours, for anyone who might not be as clever. With the logic of Solomon and the fervor of Mao, he was eons ahead of his time.

The battle lines are drawn for the most satisfying game of the year: A combined American force of three "imperialist" teachers, (or "capitalist roaders," if you prefer) versus the determined masses of the "Navigation Nation," outfitted by their real bosses in good-looking white military uniforms and deep in training for survival at sea. On the sea, as the reasoning goes, what difference does it make if you can't say "heaving" or "lifting" in English? If you can beat Manny's tests, then you can certainly figure out a way to sail to Japan. So here we go—or as they say in the Marines..."buh-vah."

Sun Tsu says "Let your plans be dark and as impenetrable as night, and when you move, fall like a thunderbolt." –The Art of War.

I would have to admit naiveté for the first month or so of my career. Manny had invited me, or urged me more accurately, to help him administer his test. I'd already done one or two and thought "What's the big deal? They're pretty good about being honest."

Just trust me on this, went the argument. The students filed in, they all sat down and prepared their desks accordingly. Manny was sure they were all sitting down before he passed out the papers with this stern nervous look on his face. He knew something I didn't know! I sat at the front desk and watched them from there like the police do when stationed at a traffic light, but while they started taking the test, Manny preferred to patrol them like a plain-clothed officer in the crowd. He looked at me like "I'm 95% sure I've got one, I'm going in... *cover me*!!" Then he takes a nose-dive across the room, thrusts his arm deep into this nervous boy's loose-fitting jacket going deep, and out he comes with this huge wadded up piece of paper.

Everyone gasps! *Dang!!* It was a bona fide cheat sheet! I immediately fall on the floor and start to bow down to the general—in my mind, at least. But I'm also struck with a single, ear-splitting thought. *"We've got work to do!"* Indeed, the Gulf of Tonkin Incident had nothing on this! This means war!!

Sun Tsu says "So it is said that if you know your enemies and know yourself, you will not be put at risk even if you have a hundred battles." –The Art of War.

Manny and Brian and I sat down and drew up a system of TSA approved tactics, whereby hands were checked, jackets removed, even the dress-code of short-sleeved white uniforms were in order. We stopped just short of using metal detectors. Cheat sheets were a little bit of a lame tactic, though, because Manny, and now our tests were all of the coded variety, but we knew that they were probably the student's most obvious line of offense. Little did we know they still had a few tricks up their sleeves.

"In the midst of chaos there is also opportunity."

"I didn't get a paper yet." "Me neither," said someone else. "*What?? I was sure you were here when everybody else walked in, how can you say you didn't get one?* Did I really miscount? Well, here you go then." I gave him another paper. Score one for the students. The extra test paper meant that all the smart student had to do was copy his answers on the paper and write the lagging friend's name on top. When grading these tests, I had to wonder when that one student that never could answer anything in class had a perfect paper. The students were going to have to do better than that if they wanted to fool me, but so was I if I wanted to justify a mark deduction.

Sun Tsu says, "Be so subtle that you are invisible. Be so mysterious that you are intangible. Then you will control your rivals' fate."

Both of us, all of us—we were learning. I did catch these kinds of tests in the future (yes, you are right, cheating became so common that I sadly have to use the plural). I started seeing a pattern where *almost* all of the answers are correct. But I also learned by observation, as the master (Sun Tsu) always said: "Never interrupt your enemy when he is making a mistake." We began studying them—even implementing Brian's DV camera.

Sun Tsu recounts, "The men of Wu and Yueh hated each other, however, encountering severe winds when crossing a river on the same boat, they assisted each other like left and right hands."

Manny had taught in China for five years, and so he had a little wisdom, but frankly, all three of us marveled intently in the paradox before us: not only was the exam system in this country fiercely competitive, but we ourselves did our best to tout the line that 'not everybody can pass.' Whatever kind of bell curve or system of rewards we tried to implement
 ͪ ͨΩͣⁿ their propensity to stick to the 'no comrade left behind' mentality.
helped each other, even if they didn't *like* each other!

Being 'capitalist roaders,' *we* were suspect, I suppose, and not particularly taken seriously. Trying our best to prepare the students for the market economy where snoozers lose, we couldn't figure out how to do it! We learned that if a smart student was far enough ahead in the game, he would even sacrifice his own grade by writing another student's name onto his only paper, or in the case of Manny's pre-labeled versions, switch papers and give the one with his name on it to a failing friend.

"Every battle is won before it is ever fought."

Manny had learned to put the names of the students on their tests beforehand after one too many went in planning to use name-switching as a tactic. But none of us thought that students would sacrifice their own grade. Of course, this didn't always happen, but it did even more in the less risky tactics students used. The atmosphere was supposed to be complete silence, but still, the act of whispering, mumbling, writing huge letters so that other students could easily catch glimpses and even outright talking was impossible to manage. We laughed so hard at the times when someone whispered "B, B, B!!!" and their friend wrote down a "P," or a "3" instead of a "C." I could see how it would be tempting to cheat this way. After all, the classes often had sixty students on these elongated desks, which meant that they had the advantage of being squeezed in close proximity—the slightest whisper could hide behind thin silence. If they could figure out how to control the *arrangement*, they could alternate the ignorant to the informed and they had a literal assembly line mechanism of correct answers.

"The art of using troops is this: When ten to the enemy's one, surround him; When five times his strength, attack him; If double his strength, divide him."

Even Julius Caesar knew this one: *"Divide and Conquer."* Because "the victory goes to the one who pays the cost," all three of us decided to donate more time to our craft and conduct our exams in two periods. That put plenty of space between them, alright.

The students had us totally sun-tzu'ed. Splitting classes created brand new opportunities to conquer us. One Vietnamese word that kept popping up in the war museum, "quyet thang," made us all scratch our heads. *Why was all this revolutionary memorabilia so quiet?* The word means "resolve to win," and the students weren't going to give up and simply study the material. They were in this thing together and they resolved to win. As Sun Tsu said best, "He will win whose army is animated by the same spirit throughout all its ranks."

We had the authority to say who came to take the test in which period, but how to cut it put us at a dilemma. "Let's put all the smart students in first, and the lower-performing ones in second period…no, wait—*do the opposite. Let the poor students go first without the smart ones' helping them.*" Knowing the lineup, the students had a day to prepare. We thought giving them their order a day early wouldn't do too much harm and was only fair to the ones who went later to have the extra hour of sleep or whatever. Haha. We just handed them twenty-four hours of strategy.

"All warfare is based on deception. Hence, when we are able to attack, we must seem unable; when using our forces, we must appear inactive; when we are near, we must make the enemy believe we are far away; when far away, we must make him believe we are near."

"I'm at the window…no one sees, give it…now! *Now, now, now!* Hurry!" One test went out the window—the poor martyrs' name on it for maybe some great honor later if all this worked out. Somebody sprinted across the street and made a photocopy, before we figured it out, which would be in about two minutes when everybody is at their desks and there's a kid with his paper missing. So someone had given him a dummy version to buy a little more time, which was like some previous test. Somehow—*gosh they were good at this,* they got the test back to the guy with a good thirty minutes of test time left. Since the poor kid didn't know anything, he was ok with it. Because the kids in second period were all the successful ones, they didn't have to much trouble memorizing the code. So in about thirty minutes, we were looking at an empty classroom, with like three stragglers who weren't in on the brilliant scheme. They, at least, all scored A's in our book.

Because we figured that two could play in the art of deception, we all decided that it was worth putting even more time and thought into our approach. Manny began crafting, not two, but even four or five different versions that looked at first glance absolutely identical! Even the first two or three answers were the same, but as you went down the row, you started to have different matches that weren't. The only way to tell the different versions apart was a little clue at the end of the opening sentence. It said: "Dear students, thank you for your hearty effort in studying for this exam. We trust that you will have a great time filling it out since you have studied so diligently. Enjoy!" On version A, it said "Enjoy!," version B said "Enjoy!!", version C "Enjoy!!!" etc. The first and last questions were the same on all the tests. Most students fell for it. At least half had the list of "A,B,C's" from a different version. Haha, caughtcha! Now what?

"Knowledge of the enemy's dispositions can only be obtained from other men."

I think all three of us were inspired by the students' high value of working together. It was, rather, the constant seat changing, whispering, writing on chairs, throwing pieces of paper on the floor, under the desk, even sticking things on the ceiling, that we hated so much. How are we ever going to teach the value of integrity for the sake of goodness, "doing the right thing, even if it hurts!" If we didn't do something, the whole nation may be in for thirty more years of the dregs. We had to keep fighting. If we wanna stop them from leaving clues in the classroom, as Sun Tzu said *"all we need do is attack some other place."* So when we did two tests, we swapped classrooms.

"Conceal your dispositions, and you will be safe from the prying of the subtlest spies, from the machinations of the wisest brains."

The students replied in kind. "All *we* need do is to throw something odd and unaccountable in his way." So the use of distractions like "Can I go to the bathroom?" could be anything from a distraction to a code (Bathroom = A, "go out" = B). Nervous tapping could be an easy code, six taps for number six, three more for "C." Some of the funniest clamor might happen at the window, like a fake decoy cheating operation—even with two proctors, distracting one gave somebody a chance to swap a paper. The opening statements became more specific: "Imagine we are now getting on a bus. The bus is not stopping. No bathrooms!!!"

In the end, we learned, as I've said, that sometimes the fight was just a big distraction to learning. After all: *"The supreme art of war is to subdue the enemy without fighting.", and "He will win who knows when to fight and when not to fight."* Everybody knows what drove every policy of Mao—win the hearts and minds of the people. So in the attitude of cooperation, Manny, the military genius, surprised us all by issuing group exams! That's right, this new tactic even caught the Vietnamese off guard. Could it be that he was getting soft? Two students are matched together to take their test together. Both receive the exact same grade. What is more, they weren't all paired at equal measure, for we knew exactly what each student might mark before they ever did. This was a gift to the struggling part of the class.

It may be that Manny had resigned himself that the students were all passing anyway, or it may be that he had some other kind of lesson altogether in mind, like 'how foolish it is to expect someone smarter to do life for you.' But the strategy worked pretty well. If two students were in constant dialogue with each other, they were far less tempted to look elsewhere for answers. When we looked at the results, astonishingly, we found them about the same as though they had taken the test individually—in other words, working in pairs didn't improve their overall performance, but whatever was lost in letting a few really awful students make it through the cracks, more was gained in giving us a more fair assessment of the ones we really thought counted—that is, the better ones. The top half of the class was finally doing their own work. We hadn't been getting an accurate look at their score because they had been so distracted trying to help their cheating comrades—or learning from them, they didn't put the full measure of potential into their own 40 minute test. This breakthrough gave me all kinds of new ideas, like calling the whole class a ship and letting them work in teams for their respective departments.

Everything was brought to naught and the great war of testing was all called for what it is—*simply the best wargame ever.* At the end of the year, our final grades for the students were all scrapped anyway and the standard way of testing was implemented by the school. It was something we all dreaded, but were fully 'invited' to participate in. We were each paired up with a different Vietnamese teacher, placed at little tables and students were placed in front of us, one-by-one and forced to read a paragraph from the book out loud and answer questions.

Another teacher named Michael warned me. "Get ready to cry. The test is emotionally trying for both teacher and student." Indeed, the poor students stepped in front of the table with knees literally knocking, or about to have a breakdown. Only the reaaally good ones looked confident, and it was this alone, probably that got them through it. As soon as one of the Vietnamese teachers sensed confidence, she or he would toss a couple of easy questions at them and smile, but the more nervous the student looked, the more it turned into a vicious interrogation. We never agreed, until we all got used to how it works. "Make sure some get blasted," and don't try to encourage everybody to fulfill their true potential, 'just blast them!' So the war of oral testing perhaps, felt like real life here, and a lot of students were left retreating to apathy or perhaps trying some form of bribery the night before. After all, they knew how real life worked. Besides, it is the only desperate tactic left when you are sitting 'naked' in front of two teachers with no friends to help you.

Ho Chi Minh said "I and others may be revolutionaries but we are disciples of Mahatma Gandhi, directly or indirectly, nothing more nothing less." He loved his people, and in the ancient line-of-thinking that went all the way back to Confucius, *to be loving is to be strict.* This philosophy was held by us, but it probably looked different. Sometimes, Manny's antics looked cruel to me, but Brian and I both knew better. Manny, more than anyone, wanted every single one of them to succeed. The harder the test and the fairer the standard the more satisfying the victory. In Manny's system, there was a chance for every one of the students to emerge as a real, verified winner. Our society seems to have tapped into this value. Getting a ticket from a policeman feels awful, but it feels awfully good not to have one, because it meant you did well. We lived and taught the principles of Solomon, which stressed rightness over pragmatism. We were trying to raise soldiers of truth, not facts. We wanted them to survive in international business, seeing in Vietnam's crystal ball their future was on a fast track to such wonderful opportunities. But one of business' worst nemeses is the erosion of trust. We wanted them to give up and join us—to trust the system, and to do the work properly. When they insisted on doing things their way, the only way to win them over in Manny's mind was to treat them like he treated ants—total annihilation.

As Sun Tsu said, "Confront them with annihilation, and they will then survive: Plunge them into a deadly situation, and they will then live. When people fall into danger, they are then able to strive for victory." From Sun Tzu, 'The Art of War.'

1 Mao Tse Tung: "Our Study and the Current Situation" (April 12, 1944), Selected Works, Vol. III

2 Tzu, Sun: The Complete Art of War, By Sun-Tzu; Sun Pin; Ralph D. Sawyer, Westview Press, 1996

Teacher, We're Camping!

"How did they ever succeed in war??" Manny looked at me and asked this when some teachers were preparing for a meeting. The scrabble of voices could not be discerned, and the blood pressures in the room were all rising. After about five minutes of absolute chaos, the teachers all suddenly fell into rank.

"We came up with a consensus and decided that you should do the third opening statement. After Mrs. Phouong over there reads a poem." Here was Vietnam in microcosm; so chaotic, and yet so organized!

The story of Vietnam's exploits in war do not carry over very well to the present day, except in the subtleties of life. Witness the slow evolution from a society entrenched in it to one the one that wants nothing to do with it. Try googling "Vietnamese" (not Vietnam) and "Military" and you'll come up with a couple things, one being video games, an old-timer American blog, and maybe a parade or two. The other being...not much. There isn't much to say, except if you dial in "Vietnamese students" and "Dien Bien Phu," you'll find quite a bit of local nostalgia here.

In the late 1990's, the transition was in full swing. There was a lot of the military war theme saturated into the students' lives and into life in general. The cheap green pith helmets were worn by every male in the north, and their usage by cyclo drivers seemed to complement the dilapidated architecture and dreary grey skies. No one can do much about the skies, but new money has cleaned up remnants of the past, and preserved what is desired. No longer do you find 'accidental' remnants of the war, but still do you see a culture that celebrates the revolution while trying its hardest not to glorify war in general. They do a pretty good job of it.

"I'm sorry to inform you, teacher, but we will not have class for the next three weeks." The reason? Military training. As teachers, we learned to expect this about once a year for each class. I ran into one occasionally on my bicycle because they would do it sometimes out in the open spaces on campus. Students were standing around in complete gear—girls in pressed olive greens would be seen manhandling these big rifles they could hardly hold straight. From a distance, we could sit on the roof and watch them marching in formation, even one time standing as a choir to sing patriotic songs.

Students would open up a little later on and tell me about some of the training games: goose stepping and wrestling or other camping type of games, though I always hoped to hear about the cool stuff I saw on ARMY commercials, ropes courses and sliding under electric wires. No, not here—that's *your* fantasy.

"But we do shoot guns!" said one girl. "They give us each a bullet, and we learn how to hold a gun the first day, and the second day we practice pulling the trigger so our bullet will count when we finally get to fire it."

I learned more about a few of the efforts to "make acquaintance with soldier's life," such as eating their version of MRE's, depriving yourself of Vietnamese TV for a week (*oooh, this is soooo hard!*), and learning how to fold bedding properly.

Of all the things we can learn from the Vietnamese, there are these protracted attempts to cultivate gratitude featured in the 'military vaca-tions.' They do exercises to remember fallen soldiers, appreciate what the previous generations have endured and generally count blessings in general. Our attempts at cultivating gratitude are empty spaces, rather than intentional efforts. One of these types of effort that I was invited into really caught my attention, at least I didn't expect to see it here. Camping.

Growing up in Arkansas, I had always loved camping. We used to go backpacking and just two years earlier, I had taken it up on myself to try and visit every state park in the region, either by backpacking, car camping, or just hiking there for the afternoon after a morning's drive. I had a closet full of gear at home. The mix of relaxation moments and positive struggle just made me feel satisfied just thinking about it. So when coming to Vietnam, this had actually puzzled me. They had this raw kind of work ethic, such beautiful scenes, with at least a few trails that were safe to walk on—the most accessible one I could think of so far had been the one at Cat Ba. But I knew it wasn't the same. Outside areas designated for tourists, there was still unexploded ordinance to think about. Walking through random peoples' backyards, as an American, was a weird concept for me, but I don't think that was the issue—people simply didn't do outdoor recreation here. It wasn't a 'thing' in this economy.

"If we were to do what you were doing," someone tried explained to me after looking at some old camping photos from Arkansas, "they would only think of some war thing we did in the past." So you can imagine how I perked up, when I found out that the students were going camping together to commemorate "student's day" and the battle of Dien Bien Phu. And they had invited me to come along!

"This is going to be fun!" I said to the courier who brought me the news. "Finally I'll be able to spend some good time with you outdoors, maybe I can come up with some old boy scout skills. Where are we going to go?"

"It's not far, teacher. Over there, actually."

"Over...

"...where?"

We opened the porch door, "You see? We are camping in the field."

"Oh."

"...well. Hey, still it will be fun. Just tell me when and where, and I look forward to, um... 'camping.'

I don't blame the Vietnamese for not wanting to remember hard times. I suppose, if you couldn't wander off the trail to go to the bathroom because who knows what kind of thing might blow up in your face, that would take some of the fun out of it. But Vietnam had not resorted to the kind of tacky attempt to drum up something as nostalgic as a "revolutionary" themed restaurant as China has lately done, and I heard later had been attempted. There is probably something in the adult's mind that wants kids to know what they'd been through. This was the drive behind the "thankfulness" sessions. Another stab at this was in an exercise called "camping," but it turns out my daydreams about doing boy scouts was a bit too advanced to be feasible with the goals of commemoration and nostalgia that were obviously a backdrop of this exercise. Communist culture likes to celebrate mostly the positive side of history, but sometimes it's so flat that a little pizazz is needed. I also noticed that students were like winding toys—when you only teach them nothing but math in these wooden pews, a rare moment of letting them free will unleash this surge of creativity and vibrancy. So I had gotten "camping" all wrong, and despite being disappointed, I found it somewhat charming in the end.

Whether or not it had much to do with the memory of war was hard to discern. I later saw it in other places—it's an across the board school-culture thing here, like homecoming queens or spelling bees somewhere else. "Camping" means kind of a secular version of the Jewish "Festival of Tabernacles," but instead of commemorating wandering in the desert, they commemorate the bygone hardships of war in the jungles. But that may be about where it stops. Students poured their hearts and souls into their booths. I guessed that there must have been a competition, but maybe not. It might just be that breath of fresh air when something is put in your care and the sky becomes the limit.

Booths were creative, but in certain bounds. They all had a tent which was placed on a spot of ground divvied up to each class, and like the Hebrew version was surrounded by a fence of some kind. The centerpiece, which received the most skilled attention was always a gate, and these were the most unique. One of the Asian-themed gates had characters, an ornate dragon cutout that had been drawn and cut over several days with bamboo frame and plastic Chinese lanterns made with red cellophane with gold trim. Another languid group may just have a basic gate with the typical icon of Ho and some Christmas lights coiled around PVC pipe. One extremely elaborate one was woven to perfection with sliced palm leaves, like a giant friendship bracelet, while other palm branches had been planted all over to give it a bit of jungle flavor. The funniest one had paper machete brick posts and belonged in a snowglobe—someone had come up with little movie theatre-style cord posts and put big colored gumdrops on each one. I started to see Maritime themes. A cool one had crane as one post and a building. It said Xay Dung, Dan Dung & Cong Nghiep (which means engineering and construction department) and had a pattern that was skillfully die cut into wood with a spangle and something abstract that I couldn't figure out. Another one had a huge wooden ship painted on it, with a giant Windows Computer as a bridge.

I finally found my class (Navigation Dept), which had created the bow of a ship out of bamboo, and crafted a similar bamboo weaving. The bowels of a big bamboo ship—though if you squinted, it might look like one of those Megashark jaws of terror that you walk into with leafy teeth.

And the cutout letters! These perfectly hand cut Styrofoam letters adorned the gate, saying: "Trai Thanh Nhien, Thi Tran TDHHH, 1953-2000, 26-3, 1-4." I asked what all the numbers meant. Those were important dates. Obviously 1953 being the victory of Dien Bien Phu, 2000 being this year. March 26th was the establishment of the Ho Chi Minh Communist Youth Union in 1931, and April 1st was the kind of V-F (Victory over France) day for Dien Bien Phu. It had nothing to do with "tell lie day," which is what my students liked to call April Fools. Posted on the tent itself, about a 12x12 tent-like structure in the middle of the courtyard, even Coca-Cola had an a stake with little red printed flags draping at the entrance. Next to it was a plaque by the door with a young cartoon sailor man with beady eyes like Tin Tin, with his green-clad girl looking into the future toward the flags. It had postered block letters saying "Long Live the Communist Party" (in Vietnamese of course).

As creative as the gateways were for each department, the inside was pretty much the same for all of these tents. The sides covered in the standard translucent pink/white/blue-striped tarp material which is universally used here, and the table too had the standard checkered red and white tablecloth. The backdrop was a dark green tarp. Little paper stars were taped up across the plastic sky. Christmas lights were mounted up on the wall in their original Styrofoam packaging, and overhead, a little hand-sewn chandelier of tiny yellow flowers wagged about in the ensuing commotion like mistletoe.

Now that I was among friends, I was eager to find out what you 'do' when you go camping like this. I waited to be invited in.

"Teacher! Yes, come, we will go camping. Come." Huy rattled off a bunch of stuff to his friend, as captain. There were a few girls invited too, and like a trade fair, there was more coming and going happening than 'dwelling' and 'communing.' Like anything in Asia, you remove your shoes, and try to keep from being nudged off the 8x8' bamboo mat which is also the same one used everywhere—the one with red painted edges and a rose in the middle that always puts red streaks on my khaki pants. There were some classmates standing around and the horseplay was in session and so the occasional thump to a post or a wall made the chandelier tinkle.

"Teacher, do you see our house? What do you think?" I was impressed and I told them so. Heaps of traditional cakes were piled on the table. And the obvious centerpiece, I don't know where they got this—a huge bust of Ho Chi Minh—with a plate of bananas (probably for Ho and not for us). Flowering planted Ming Dynasty pots were neatly arranged here and there in the corners, and the guitar reverently rested beside Ho's ever approving proud stone shoulders. Other tents had TVs on the tables and those fuzzy Christmas sparkle ropes, but the standard arrangement made walking into all the tents pretty much the same experience.

Recently, I was curious if these festivals still happen, and I found some online. One of the descriptions said the following: *The camping festival is a helpful, healthy playground, contributing to strengthening friendships and the necessary skills of students. It is also a great event for students and pupils to meet and exchange studying experiences.* Apparently, they still take place quite often, with themes like "teacher's gratitude" and "From Dien Bien Phu to Homeland's Sea and Island." March 26th (the Youth League anniversary) is seemingly the common denominator, and featured activities of late range from martial arts, to counter-terrorism and hostage rescue and skills, and even high-speed Motorbike-driving workshops. "Maybe camping is pretty cool stuff after all!" But for us, the items on the billet included singing, dancing, and alcohol

"Teacher's here. We do wine now!" Others appeared out of nowhere. "Wine! Wine wine wine!" So much for a "helpful, healthy playground." I tried to divert them by asking if they knew any songs. "Teacher, yes! Sing us a song! We will listen." I thought there's no way they could be serious about the wine. At a school function!! They were. It was still happening and some of them already had bright red faces, from earlier I guess. They were also gettin' rowdy.

"I will play," said somebody to my rescue, after whatever I tried to sing didn't suit their fancy. A skinny kid I didn't know, grabbed the guitar, and started playing talentedly. The other students joined in with a burst of loud. It was a war ditty, "red music," they like to say, with a Russian choral kind of flavor. I liked the kind of sound of it, they were all singing it at the top of their lungs, and I hummed along, imagining I was in a play about Russian cartoon sailors. "Teacher, ...dance!" The tone of the music eventually changed to more of a rhumba, this time from a boombox that I hadn't seen under the table, and we were all lured into dancing wildly like among baboons in the novel "Lord of the Flies."

I forced myself to stay in this environment for about an hour, but when the students had gotten so drunk that it didn't really matter, I gave into my beckoning home, which had been calling me for almost the whole past hour. Fairly socialed out, I detoxed in a good book or something quiet. But as darkness settled, I looked out from my balcony over a glistening carnival scene and a curious thought came to my mind. *"I wonder how many days this goes for?"* There were folk games of some kind going on, though very foreign—one person tagging another and running from wall to wall, and at one end of the field someone was preparing a campfire for all the students. I asked Khanh and Chinh when I found them if they wanted me to sleep here.

"Sleep here? What do you mean?" asked Khanh.

"Well, you are camping, aren't you? Don't you all sleep out here?"

"No no!" laughed Chinh. "Camping you no sleep. Just dancing."

"What do you mean, 'you dance all night, or you go home to sleep?' "

"Yes, that." Said Khanh. Thank God I don't have to camp for real, I finally conceded.

I came back down refreshed, and hoped maybe their intoxication 'phase one' had worn off a bit (how do they ever do motorcycle speed workshops in this setting?). Everyone was pretty much ok. The evening had a more tempered feel to it, like the campfire I might have always wanted, though the agenda was being 'controlled' by Mr. Kien, who was the Young Communist Youth Director here. It wasn't so different from a Cub Scout campfire, but all the language was above my current range. After a while, realizing that my presence could have been a distraction, I retreated back into the shadows.

The next day, I looked and saw the empty field, revelry gone and students cleaning up the mess. I imagined what the morning would have been like if it were not a Sunday, with the familiar "mot hai mot hai mot hai (1,2,1,2)," and the students groggily jogging with a hangover. Weeks and months later, I would think of their ingenuity when properly mobilized and wonder how I could harness the same kind of creativity in learning English, but it often proved hard without Mr. Kien's endorsement. When I finally came back and gave them copies of the pictures I had taken of them, they were extremely grateful and wanted me to sign each one. As far as war tourism, there was about as much talk about that as any American talking about their last Fourth of July party might mention our wars, but the barbecue and beer sure were great. No wonder they mix up the words "Uncle Ho" and alcohol! The school year was soon to end at this point, and later we had our going away parties and the like. The students asked me, worriedly, if I were coming back.

"Of course I will, but I don't know if I will teach your class or not."

"That's great, teacher!" said Khanh. Someone else nodded happily. "We'll try our hardest to study English!" said someone else. So we talked for a while about the memories of the year and all the things that were yet to see, the upcoming summer and year ahead. "We'll go to Halong Bay, or nearby Cat Ba Island. We can take you for the Buffalo Festival."

"I look forward to it, of course I do."

"And when you come back, teacher, we're definitely going camping."

Calling Class 911

The greatest gift we ever received in Vietnam was a shiny glazed black flower vase. For numerous occasions, if flowers were handed to us, we knew exactly what to do. "Go and grab the vase." It was seven weeks into our second year of teaching, and Vietnam's biggest civil holiday of the year after Tet, *Vietnamese Teachers Day*, had come.

5:00 am. A knock at the door.

Students.

"Greetings on the occasion of International Teacher's Day, our dear teacher. Please accept these gifts in our great appreciation of your service." I was handed two bundles of red roses—not being too coherent, I went to find that the vase had already been filled.

"Vase's full. Early birds had come last night already. They have a lot of teachers to see, usually starting with their primary school teachers." Manny had a point. So, what to do with these? Vietnam Teachers' Day hadn't been so big last year, but this year we have last year's classes *and* this year's classes. We looked around and found our laundry tubs. Filling them with water, we waited for the great and imminent tidal wave of love.

A knock at the door.

Hey, it's class 911! At least, maybe, twelve of them—"Greetings, on the occasion of Vietnam Teacher Day we bring you these flowers. Please accept as a gift of our appreciation." In the tub they go! There were others coming up the stairs. I could hear them.

"Brian, Manny! We're going to need more tubs." There were no tubs. We started to look through the trash, where we found emptied plastic water bottles.

"You know, these are so cheap, why don't we buy a bunch more and empty them into our larger empty jug, so we can use them as vases. So we had gotten to work, accumulating a forest of roses that was beginning to fill the room. More footsteps. Oh boy! Here come more! International Teacher Day and birthdays were Vietnam's answer to the Passadena Rose Bowl Parade. And it was *all* for us.

"We have finally sorted out the classes for you this year," said Mrs. Thanh with a bit of a wink. Again, we had arrived to Vietnam to be given the ten days of delay. We sat down to receive our assignments. For me, another navigation class—this time Freshmen, who started this year in 1999. The year was indicated by the "9" plus "1" for navigation plus "1" for being the first of two classes. 911 it was. I wondered if they knew the emergency phone number was 911 in America. But after teaching "seven-eleven" last year, I figured a freshman class might be a great change. Start the year off right we could, with Mr. Bean.

Whenever I couldn't keep their attention, I had stepped a bit outside of my personality and refashioned myself into something like Jim Carrey. When I did this, the students sometimes muttered "Mr. Bean, you're Mr. Bean!"—the closest thing they could associate with any kind of exaggerated antic was Rowan Atkinson's international performances, called "Mr. Bean." Taking my cue from what I knew of the show, I went along with it in small doses, trying to keep their attention when they were at their most restless. However, I was also going to tackle the lack of English vocabulary more seriously and more head on this year, assuming without a doubt that if they covered a wide-range of English last year, they really would this year. At least class 711 had a year behind them, some of these may have no exposure to English whatsoever.

Compiling the best of the previous year, I had already started working on materials that would meet this challenge. Toward the end of the previous year, I had gone a little bit off the deep end with creativity, and saw the need to tighten things up. Sensing that kinesthetic hands-on activities were more fun for the students, I had created these fake engines out of Styrofoam, film containers, and other junk I found—making some of the students cry. Not the kind of cry that is merely complaining, but the kind of cry that might happen if I had ripped up someone's test in front of his peers. "Teacher, this is not possible to *do*!!," was followed by some kind of tears.

"Come on, guys. It's not that hard. I tried to make it easy—just read the instructions." Basically, I had given them some version of technical instructions and they were supposed to figure them out and demonstrate their understanding on these model engines. Despite being creative, and a lot more interesting than grammar drills in my opinion, the complete bewilderment of the students at this very strange-looking exercise last year had led me back to doing simple things again. When I saw how they were finally tested at the end, I too was pretty done with the complex use of English to solve what I thought were real problems they might face and was more interested in centering in on the first said problem—how to face the final. It wasn't about using your brain, it was about knowing the words.

Learning language myself had tuned me into their need for ridiculous amounts of repetition. I went slower than I thought anyone would need to go. We repeated the same words every day.

"What is this again?"

"Surge, teacher." My flash cards were big, beautiful and hand drawn. Yes—drawn. I had drawn perhaps three hundred verb flashcards. Verbs, not nouns, because nouns are almost always easy to point to, describe, and see and understand. Verbs are more abstract, and so I drew pictures of the verbs and pulled them out daily in the form of big flashcards. "That's right—surge! This one?..."

"Pull."   "Push."   "Open."   "Close."

Then, we go through them again in past tense, telling a sentence, asking a question, the combinations were varied and I decided that between last years' handouts and these, I could fill half the class time. For the higher-level students, I would ask them to make a sentence, for the lower ones, the word was enough. It wasn't any use diving right into *English for Seafarers,* because they didn't know the words yet. Now...*how* to keep the good English kids from dominating the struggling kid next to them? Groups!

Class 911 was my first attempt at creating permanent groups. I gave each of the groups names like Whales ("Sea Elephant" in Vietnamese), Seals ("Sea Dog"), Starfish, Dolphins, Squids, Penguins, and Hammerheads. Groups were split somewhat according to skill level, so I could at least work with them in tandem and keep the good ones from doing all the work for those who had less English ability.

With lots of work, careful attention to detail, and vigilant planning around scheduled international football matches on TV, we had pretty much smooth sailing on into November, when Teachers Day suddenly arrived.

"Today we will talk about holidays. I will write some of them on the board." Manny and I did teach some of our religious holidays—it is important to us to detail some of the context of our personal faith, and this seemed like an appropriate time to do it, but we avoided these when it wasn't close to one of them and focused on minor holidays. "Saint Patrick's Day, Veteran's Day..."

"...Teacher, can you help me finish this sentence?" A kid in the front row held up his book, which had nothing to do with holidays. It was a grammar exercise from some night class he was taking: *"Skip and Hal____ (have learnt / will have been learning) arithmetic when they enter college."*

"If you come to my room, I'll help you with it later, now have you written the holidays from the board onto your paper yet?"

"Yes teacher," he grinned showing me an empty notebook.

"TeachercanIgoout?" said one kid.

"Teacher, you didn't write 'Teachers Day.' " Another boy stood up with a marker mustache on his face.

"TeachercanIgoout?" repeated the first kid.

"Yes, teacher's day, but that's not a day we have in the West."

"Teacher, what about chismas?" said another."

"What about International Womans Day?"

I had an idea. "We'll do 'Vietnam Teachers Day' as a focus, everybody write five things that teachers do on Vietnam Teachers' Day!" I thought I might do a little research, because we had less than a week left for the big holiday.

Answers ranged: Giving presents, writing poems, cooking (…cooking?), flowers, flowers and more flowers. Singing songs and studying harder. The last wasn't happening, and come to think of it, I had no excuse for not preparing plenty of plastic water bottle vases on the day.

What the students forgot to write about was the long assembly.

"Do you think they are close to being done yet?" I whispered to Brian in as low a voice as I thought would transfer, as we sat for about the eighteenth speech.

"No look. In the program, see here?" There was actually a printed program. Well, we were on number three.

"Number 9 is lunch, I think. Number 8 is somebody's speech. Yep. Five more numbers to go." We couldn't talk too loud because the students were all being quiet. Whoever was talking was rambling on and on and using a piece of paper in his hand. There was a TV man who had a large camera nestled over his shoulder who was standing up in the speakers face. I looked around more at the students. They were all sitting indian-style in their perfect starched uniforms, almost unflinching as military, and I marveled at the inconsistencies in life here.

"Wait, I think it's moving faster now," I said hopefully, but the next speaker started to spread her note papers out on the podium and organize them with paper clips.

"What?"

"The program."

"Oh boy," we said. "This is going to be a while. Let's do lesson planning in our minds."

Lunch was amazing, and it came with specially printed teacher's day satchels, with matching pens and a lovely bonus.

"Actually, I would have to say the assembly was *quite* nice," we all nodded to each other with new perspective. In some ways, being paid to sit and listen is easier than holding the attention ourselves. And the lunch was one of those that just keeps coming—a true *bona fide* Chinese banquet. The female teachers were all dazzling in their ao dai dresses and we took picture after picture after picture! When I returned to class 911 the next day, they were still in festive spirits and some of them had even prepared notes and cards. When they saw my new satchel, they all clapped. Somehow I didn't remember any of this level of sophistication from the year before. Regardless of my performance, I felt loved just to fill the office. Whatever they were doing to make underpaid teachers feel the love—it was working on me.

New classes brought with them new faces, friends, talents and locales. I tried to treat all my students equally, but since friends are what the heart needs, I broke down with two new exceptions. These were Kha and Manh.

Kha and his friend Hung made a special visit when some of the magic of Teachers' Day had worn off. Kha was a model student and much more— he charmed me right away with the way he looked like Morgan Freeman to me and always said "Yes, suh," like a southern man, perhaps a Hoke Colburn or an Ellis 'Red' Redding. I don't think that he was actually saying it intentionally, it just sounded like that way and it charmed me quite a bit. For Manh, it was his pure heart that felt like enthusiasm for everything. He looked like one of those handsome soldiers on the cartoon propaganda posters that were all over town. When Kha or Manh or other closer friends ever came for a visit, I always felt excited and accommodating, and so I decided they were more genuine friendships and didn't mind treating them like friends—especially since, again, they were good students and their performance did merit anything that looked like special attention. And they both had these *sidekicks*, I called them, who came about every other time. In both cases, their friends didn't have quite the English or the consistency they had, but I liked them too. For Kha it was 'hardcore Hung,' and for Manh it was 'smiling Thang.' I swear, that boy had a permanent smile that never wiped away. These four were added into the mix of the other several guys who I considered more in the friend category.

"Hey Kha and Hung," I said, pouring tea—finally having mastered this part of the hospitality ritual—and what number of teacher am I to visit? "Number three. We visit our secondary school teachers first."

"We don't have teachers' day in America. I wonder if people would even remember who their elementary school teachers are."

"You don't have teacher's day, are you speak true? How do you tank your teachers, teacher?"

"At the end of the year, I guess. We always say we do it by giving them an apple, but I never see anybody doing that, either."

"I wrote a poem for you. It's in Vietnamese, sorry. You can read it?"

I found out pretty early that Kha was a talented poet. He had once told me his name, Kha, like mine, was unusual. "My father's name was Kha, and my grandfather's name was Kha, with no tone." And he liked penning poems. This isn't too unusual in Vietnam, but his poems were pretty good. Coming out of China, Vietnamese is a very poetic language, and there is no end to the amount of puns and parallels you can pen by shifting tones around.

"You really should print your poems in a magazine. I tried reading the last one you gave me, but some words weren't in the dictionary. By the way, what does the name mean again, the one that you keep signing at the bottom?"

"Hương Đồng Gió Nội"

That was Kha's pen name. He assured me it was hard to translate, but it means something like "The Wind Roars Evermore,"—just this year I googled it and saw that a movie had been released under that title in 2013, which had been translated into a more boring English title, "Better and Better." It may then be an idiom that denotes some kind of improving momentum.

I did remember receiving this poem, but I just assumed that it had been completely lost, simply having been scrawled onto a piece of scratch paper. Entombed in a landfill. Imagine my surprise and delight, then, just last night as I was preparing for this article, I dug into a box and found two of Kha's poems! Here is one of these, called "Neu (If)," as follows:

Nếu có thể là con suối nhỏ

Ngày và đêm vẫn sóc sách theo nguồn

Cho cô bé mà lòng anh yêu mến

Tắm mát lành trong dòng nước trong xanh

Nấy có thể anh là bình minh

Của một sang sau đêm dai tăm tối

Để đơi anh, đơi em thểm trang mới

Để em đăm chin trong hạnh phúc bao la

Và có thể anh tan ra thành mây khói

Tận trời cao anh vẫn hướng theo về

Nơi phố nhỏ có người anh yêu mến

Vẫn cần cù bên sách vở sớm hơn

Nhưng có thể anh chỉ là hạt cát bụi

Nhơ vô vàn hạt cát nhỏ quanh ta

Và khi đó cuộc đời anh vô nghĩa

Biết em còn...

Cô bé của anh ơi?

Hương Đồng Gió Nội

Translating poetry is not my strong point, but with google translate as a starting point, I did some tidying up, and came up with the following—but I sure could use Kha's help:

If there could be a small stream

Day and night she always embraces it

Her heart goes out to her lover,

She bathes in the water so cool, so blue.

Could he be as the coming of the dawn

Following a long night of darkness?

To wait for him, sometimes she adds another page

Allowing her to maintain her blissful, hopeful state.

And would he suddenly dissolve into a plume of smoke

Amidst the driving sky?

On the small street where once he loved her,

It's still there buried in a book, as before.

But maybe it is nothing but a grain of sand,

Amidst the many small particles of sand all around us.

And then this life would seem pointless

Still I know ...you still belong to me, do you not?

As my students are very fond of saying: "Please correct me if you can!!"

"Are you and Hung going to go home this weekend?" I asked after we had done poems.

"Hung is going to his homeland. But I want you to come with me to Thai Binh, maybe next month. *Are you ok?*"

"Now *that* is more like it!" I thought it to myself. November was the prime season with good weather, but December would begin to bring in the chilly season I also really liked, and I could think of nothing better to do than going to a new town I had never been to before—much further down into the Red River Delta, to ancient Vietnam. I now had something terrific to look forward to.

Thai Binh is one of several cities located near each other—Nam Dinh sits on one side of the canal and Thai Binh on the other, to the north are Hung Yen and Phu Ly. Further south is Ninh Binh. Unlike these places, Thai Binh is not at all on the railway, so it requires a bus, with special knowledge of where to hop off. Only the old tin-can-styled local buses go there. Kha's village is actually a nondescript village called Cat Bi (Khu Chung Cu Cat Bi), in Hai An district, a few miles before the bus enters Thai Binh. Of all the villages I had been to so far, I found this quaint and compact little village to be the most interesting one so far (and that's saying a lot). The landscape is not as dramatic as Ninh Binh and just about everything West and South of it, or north of Haiphong. Instead, it's very flat but it is the bread-basket for Hanoi and so very agricultural. Layers of history are still evident, with big French churches on the outer rim, and wooden Buddhist pagodas on the inner rim. At the epicenter was the perfectly preserved Keo Pagoda.

The Keo Pagoda was the only thing noted in a single paragraph of *Lonely Planet* as being "worth seeing" here. I would take that to be directed at total outsiders—but having Kha at my helm meant that everything was worth seeing. When we hopped off the bus, we were greeted by a relative, who told both of us to hop onto his motorbike. It was already fired up. There was a recent ban on more than one passenger on motorbikes, but rules like that would take years to fully reach these parts, as would any proscription for a helmet. I obeyed. Most of the men wore the green army 'pith' helmet as fashion, anyway. Crossing the divide into the village, we raced through a large flat field toward the horizon. Immediately in, we twisted through a mouse-maze of turns, every corner turned posed a question. "What are they drying here on the roadside?" – "What is the meaning on all these signs that say *"thit meo?"* Do they really serve cat here?" "What is that monument we just passed?" "How old must that building be?" "What are they doing near the tree?" "Do you ever play football there in that field?" "Those are not real bombshells, are they?" "Is that a Dong-Ho painting on the wall?" – All of these questions would have to wait, my cheeks were pressed up against the back of Kha's neck and I was holding on tightly to keep from slipping off the back of the bike. A quick flyby of each doorway revealed a clean courtyard, many were occupied by kids. Every eye that caught my passing snapped up—I was not an everyday occurrence here. I was just as transfixed on them and everything else as they were on me. There was an untouched feel to this place that was instantly noticeable. Now, thinking back, it is one of just a few places that felt like a time capsule. It almost felt like I wasn't supposed to be there.

We rolled into a café, which had bright blue walls, and a view of a busy intersection through an extra-wide window that functioned equally as a transaction counter. Mostly bicycles were passing. On the wall was indeed a Dong Ho (folk painting) and candy items that were of local make. In fact, everything was home-grown and local—a big contributor to the feel of timelessness. Coca-cola was an exception, but it was not flaunted, just a stack of bottles sitting in the corner in cases. Several neighbors were there and all of them interested in me. The storekeeper didn't know what to tell them until being informed by Kha. We sat down for a drink, of course, with Kha's cousin-brother. And we talked of trivialities, maybe 'till somebody down the road had approved my coming. You sometimes had the feeling that a great machine was in motion, and all we saw was the face of the clock.

With no warning, Kha popped up mid-sentence. "We go now, teacher?"

We rolled into the homestead—not at all unlike the others I had visited, with a spacious pond, neck-high fence surrounding a stone courtyard, an outhouse, potted plants, a caged-bird, banana trees to one side, several other trees, including tall coconut trees looking down on everything like angelic guardians. Kha's father, a character, greeted us at the gate and took all my stuff—ushered me in for tea. The inside was dazzling blue tiled and clean. There was no altar, but later I found out that a huge one upstairs had been given its own room. It was the most exquisite one I had ever seen at the time, and some of the food was brought down from up there. There was a picture of a young man who could have been Kha, but obviously a relative from an earlier time who left too early. Quite a few relatives were already in a kind of dance, making ready for lunch. I will not dwell here, except to say that the food was unique.

"What is this kind of pork? It's very sweet. Delicious, actually."

"Dac san, teacher," said Kha—saying the word for local specialty.

"I know, but..." pressing foolishly.

"Meo," said a sister.

When Kha took me to Keo Pagoda, I knew I had found something very special. In a way, it seemed like the perfect place for Kha to come from, with his poetic talent and knack for Vietnamese heritage. This is one of the places where the ancient Vietnamese drum had been unearthed—the oldest part of the country. Kha not only showed me poems, but he liked to tell stories from the past as well. What impressed me most were the remoteness and rawness of this place. For one thing, it was so far from anything so people didn't come here much, no matter what *Lonely Planet* said. What that meant was that no attempt had been made whatsoever to "clean it up" for tourism. It was, and felt, just as it might have always looked. The whole complex was entirely earth-toned, extravagant—the bell tower felt brittle, wooden, and carved down to the minutia. I touched the gorgeous wooden doors, afraid that the grease on my fingers might cause it to melt. I don't know how old it was—Kha said three hundred years—but laying eyes on this gem that never got visited, so deep in Vietnam, it made me feel a little bit like a researcher, or an archeologist. Most of us can't say we have a world-heritage-quality site right around the corner from our yard.

I wandered around there with Kha for over an hour, but didn't want to leave. Not to give too much credit to a pagan temple—but I looked at Kha and asked, "Do they have a festival here?" Yes, did they ever! Could we come? Of course, teacher.

The weather turned from mild to blustery on this mid-December day, and Kha and I hustled back to his home to think about how we would make it home. Northern Vietnam has this wintery season that reaches its height in later January when Tet happens, but the cold had not fully arrived. A few people could be seen donning sweaters, black leather jackets and scarves when we boarded the bus though. Being back on the bus felt more like the present, but without a trace of city-culture on the bus. Rather than wait at the junction where we had been dropped off, Kha's brother had taken us to the actual station, and the bus was almost full. As I climbed on the bus, I was thankful for Kha, for this new class I was teaching now that had also produced other prodigies like him, for a part of Vietnam that had not yet been filmed into a Discovery Channel special, and for the chance to see these new places before the rest of the world.

Tomorrow I would teach again with new vigor, feeling for the first time a little bit attached to a specific town. This was no more "my town" than Hanoi was, but I thought about how my 'home' was growing. It was no longer just a room, a street or a city. It was a whole region that included Thai Binh and who knows how many more places remained to be seen in this giant open void between Hanoi and distant Hue.

Cat Ba On a Shoestring

If we were playing the televised game of "Survivor," I was sure I would be the *first* one voted off the island. Here's the story.

"Hey, I have a great idea!" I told Khanh. "Let's all go to Cat Ba."

"Uh, that's great, teacher. But..." Khanh looked down almost shamed. I could tell he wanted to say he didn't have the money.

"Don't worry Khanh. I've *got* this. You don't have to bring anything. Just find Chinh and Thanh and tell them too ok? And Son if he wants."

These were my "Gang of Four," the fellows I'd come to really enjoy being around ever since the day I'd gone out to play many endearing games of soccer with them. This was my second year so I wasn't their official teacher anymore, we'd grown closer, playing ball, doing karaoke, English clubs, even learning cultural stories on Saturdays with pancakes. I loved slipping away to Cat Ba, but every time I did it, I always thought "It's so remote and idyllic out here, how fun it would be to bring a group of friends!" So I had saved up some cash and I was pretty sure I had enough to comfortably bring even as many as five or six guys out here. I had some students who were girls now, but I thought it would be less complicated, culturally, if I kept it to the guys.

They were all game except Son, so we chose a day and headed out. On the Saturday morning, I showed up at Khanh's door at 4:48 in the morning. It was eerily quiet. I had brought my bicycle and it always felt so weird to be out at such an early time. The roads are light enough, but the fact that there are a few roamers out, and sometimes the cleaners are out that early, so it gives it the feel of desolation even more than if every soul were completely absent. Khanh lives down a tiny side alley so it was even scarier, but as I squeaked up on my bike, I saw that his door was open, and the metal grating was pulled, as though it had been kept that way all night. I whispered into the dark room.

"Khanh!"

Again, "Khanh!"

I felt movement in the room and groggily the familiar face of Khanh's dad showed up.

"Khanh, oi!!!" He shouted, shattering the night. There were a couple clatters and Khanh came down looking fairly fresh and ready.

"Hello, Hayden." He said.

"Did you sleep well?"

"No, Hayden. Every time I have to up early, I never sleep...well."

I related.

"What about Thanh and Chinh? Do you think they are awake?" As if to answer, I heard a motorbike hum down the alley.

"They come."

We piled up on two motorbikes with some cousin of Khanh's I had never met and his dad.

Gulp! "Are they going too?" I wondered. But it turned out that they were taking us to the pier and had come along to bring home the bikes. So we rolled off, the four of us on the back of their two bikes, and the familiar good feelies started to rumble in my stomach as I paid for four fares to Cat Ba, 256.000 dong, or 17 dollars.

Two of them had never been to even Halong Bay and all four were new to Cat Ba Island. It had only fairly recently garnered general appeal, particularly to the Vietnamese who tended to travel for the bells and whistles, and may have felt the enticements to Cat Ba underwhelming. Indeed, I knew that many of her secrets had to be experienced to be appreciated.

"You guys are going to love it. We can take a boat ride around the bay and see almost everything we can see on an ordinary trip to Halong Bay. But in Cat Ba, we can hike in the National Park. Did you bring shoes?"

Everyone had. We were set.

"Let's get snacks!" I said, first treating them to a bowl of breakfast, and then we gathered up bags of apples, packaged twinkie cakes, and expensive but gross half-incubated eggs.

"And there are some nice beaches, and if we want, we can visit a military cave and also a tower with great views." I didn't tell them about the rainbow or the monkeys from a previous visit.

Chinh and Thanh were excited and talked away with each other as I tried to comprehend, while our boat tooted and started moving. The sun was coming up quick and was already painting the ships in golden orange tints. They were pointing out all the things they had learned as we slowly exited Haiphong's port zone. They were commenting on the towers and ships. They had been out on Vimaru's training vessel called the Sea Star.

"Tell me," I asked them, "would they ever let me on board the Sea Star?"

"I don't know," mused Khanh. "They have very high securities. Maybe they will let you. I shall ask our Navigation teacher and we will take you!" That latent dream never came true for my whole stay, but it continuously made for good conversation. I knew all about the Sea Star because of descriptions in our book *English For Seafarers*.

As customary, we all found ourselves lulled to sleep by the boat's engine: clackity-clackity-clack. When I awoke, I was slightly startled to see that we had already come near the island. I went out to find the guys on top of the boat again with their head in a game of cards. "Different strokes,..." I always thought, as I would have been more engaged in the scenery and

I would have made a mental note about that and Vietnamese but then thought foreigners are just as bad. I can't stop looking at this wondrous scenery. I was excited about the prospect of visiting the National Park with them. Very excited.

"We need to choose a hotel," I said, as we disembarked. "They are pretty much all the same, but let's look for a nice, clean one. Do you want to go in and check without me—maybe you can get a better price!" They were all too willing to work the prices. Each one went into a different one. When we convened secretly out under a tree, we compared prices. Sure enough, they were pretty similar.

"Let's go for the better one!" I said, trying to break them of their tightwad habits. "We'll live it up. You are very special."

So we checked into the upstairs room of the hotel I had used with my parents on their trip which was still lingering in my memory. The room was clean and there were too huge beds so I thought that I wouldn't wake up squished in with a bunch of guys, because they are used to sleeping hang-hai-hang-ba (side by side in rows) when conditions mandate it.

We all started making nests of stuff, pulling things out of our bags and organizing our huddle for the next two days. And that is when I stopped there in my tracks.

"One, two."

"Three, Four, Five, Six."

"....Sssssssssee-venn...

"Eh, Ekh, Ek..." not bringing myself to say eight.

Suddenly, I went back to preschool.

"One. Twwwooooooo....."

"Treee?" Sounding Adam Sandler's falsetto. My mind was racing a quantum speed. We did not have enough money. I had been counting the green 50.000 dong notes, meaning that I had eight of them. As you may recall, the boat required five to make 250. I thought we could shave the six off the top if we tried. That left only three. The hotel was cheap, but we had foolishly not chosen the cheapest, not realizing, so it was going to relieve us of one hundred and twenty dong.

"That leaves thirty thousand dong." My face grew pale. Two dollars.

"*What, ...you ok? Hayden?..... No problem? Some problem?*"

I responded with a shaky and high pitched voice...

"(wheeze)---"

My eyes dilated. I began to feel clammy. They guys looked at each other a little confused.

I regained my composure. "*Ok guys.* Let's see if you have any money at all. I've totally underestimated how much we need here. I'm really sorry." I was rummaging through my stuff like a cat in a litterbox.

"What, ...you no *money* teacher?"

"Listen. Yes. *I no money*!!!" I said in an agitated way.

"Oh." Khanh's face suddenly became caucasian as mine turned red.

"Teacher, I found some money!!" said Chinh.

"Thank God!" I moaned, feeling relief.

"I was going to give my sister. You can pay me back. Twenty thousand, see?"

So now we had three and a half dollars.

"Ok, what about you, Thanh? Do you have any money?"

"*No teacher. I no happy. No money.*" I swear these are the only words he knows.

Khanh just shook his head with his lips firmly pursed, his gaze pierced and mind also running. He hadn't brought any money at all. Not a dong.

"Well, we have enough money to pay for the trip back, and enough for the hotel. But except for that, we're on our own with fifty thousand dong."

"Izz ok, teacher. We can do. Let me see *all* money" said Khanh realizing by now that I was no longer any good for anything and shoving some promotional brochures and a menu off the table to clear it. We laid out each precious bill side by side, and I searched my pockets.

"Look, *I found eight more!*" I squealed! A few cents, but I laid it out reverently, smoothing it out with my hand where it had been wadded up as change. Khanh likewise moved it beside the others.

They began to chatter loudly, even arguing and as each of these three stated their case, they moved the bills around like battlements of war. No, put *this* one *here*. No dummy, he needs that for the hotel. Here, let's put *this* for food and *that* for the boat. Let's just pay the boat guy back when we get home.

"Hey, what about *that*?" I spoke up in English, "Do you think the boat will take an i.o.u?"

"*What* teacher?"

"Oh, um. Do you think, the boat will let us pay after?"

"Nooo, teacher. Many Vietnamese will *cheeting*!" He had a point there.

"Wait don't!!!—" I gasped as Chinh had reached for one of the remaining twinkies.

"Ok, then," I sighed, as though I still had *any* say in this matter, "maybe we should go out there now and try to buy the boat ticket before somebody steals our only cash."

We tried to bargain—after the fact—with the hotel manager which never works and they didn't budge. I wouldn't either, because the hotel already felt to me like a real steal, and maybe the manager was a little upset that they hadn't mentioned me in their original deal. I was ecstatic that we had the foresight to use that strategy, so we insisted on paying the hotel up front in case they changed their mind. The boat had left and the ticket office closed, so we put the whole 256.000, with the six coming from the extra eight I had discovered, into the safest place we could think of. That was a case holding my glasses. Then, we went back up to the war room to lay it out again, and spend another season talking about it.

"Well, I guess we have plenty of time, now!" I thought stupidly. Khanh's attitude was really optimistic, so I tried riding that wave, though it felt wimpy, like surfing in Do Son baby ones.

"What will we do?" I asked feebly. I was feeling despair, but this was normal life for them.

"We go to *market*!" said Khanh.

"Ok, let's ok."

"No, you no go teacher," said Chinh. "We need good price!"

After I had emotionally flagellated myself in the room for a while, they all came back with a big bag full of breads, lots of vegetables, instant noodles, crackers, more packaged twinkies and even little Nutella packets.

"Where did you get all *this*?? Wait—

I paused. "How much is left?"

They held out an amazing twenty five thousand dong.

"You got all this for twenty-five thousand dong?"

"Twenty-seven teacher," said Khanh, reminding me of the two that hadn't gone to the boat fare from the money in my pocket.

"Well, this isn't exactly the shrimp dinner I wanted to buy," I suddenly corrected myself for being so bourgeoisie. "We're still going to have fun out here, we have each other still, so we don't need to spend a lot of money. And we'll make our own fun! I was suddenly feeling better now that I knew that we were going to be able to eat something. I could see a gleam in Khanh's eye. He had saved the day and we all knew it.

We all decided that we were going to blow 4/5ths of our savings on the beach. It had a 5.000 dong per person fee, and with the most expensive thing, the ride to the National Park, now out of the question, the beach was deemed necessary to make Cat Ba a vacation. But we wouldn't go too early or too late. We would go at an optimal time to spend three or four hours. And I almost gleeked at someone's idea to fake the karaoke by singing loudly over the TV. We had fun thinking of other free holiday activities. Going back to the market to pick up girls, though I don't know what we could offer apart from free English lessons. How about offering to do yardwork in exchange for a ride around the island? Go door to door interviewing the few inhabitants for a survey of their favorite revolutionary hero. Or playing soccer in the street with a squashed can and see if anybody comes out to play?

In the end, all these were squashed for a hike up the local hill to the revolutionary monument that looked like a satellite base, but on closer observation just turned out to be a mediocre sculpture.

"Look, we can see down there far."

"We could still hike there for free. Though it goes quite far."

Let's do it, we decided, so we went down the hill, but after passing a couple homes, it was clear that it was going to be wild road hiking which ceased being fun, so we marched back home. It was a little bit of a bummer that we could only go to the beach once and there wasn't any beach where you could stick your toes in other than the main one. I also wished I'd brought games like UNO, but we did have the deck of cards they were playing before. In my mind was the fact that I didn't know the rules to all their varied cultural card games. Their problem was "how do you play any of our games without money?" We compromised by pretending, and so that weekend I got to learn quite a few interesting games before we broke out the first of our precious bread and shared a nutella package.

Our visit to the beach worked out ok. We all got in the water and waded out, relishing the wet with new appreciation. We buried them in the sand, and somebody put beautiful breasts of sand on Khanh when he wasn't looking. We meandered slowly along the extended walkway going around the mountain—it's the one that was later destroyed in the storm and rebuilt recently—but at that time, it was this amazing addition that my parents had also experienced on a later trip. We went out on it and felt the cool air, fearing a little that the guys would get bored and then we would leave to the hotel and be *more* bored! I was amazed at their ability to be relaxed with no dough! I wondered how they did it.

We did go back to the market to look for girls, but nobody wanted the free lessons. We didn't need karoke to sing songs in the starlight, up on top of the building were we could look out on the sunset that night. The next morning we would go home, so we slurped up every bit of the feast we had purchased, saving only the noodles for breakfast.

"You guys are such good sports. Thank you for keeping your head up!" I said.

"*What*, teacher?"

"You did well not to spend money!" I said.

"Oh. Yes, we no choice," he said.

"You're right. But you had a good attitude!"

"Ahh," said Khanh, probably understanding.

Thanh came up and offered us some oranges and chewing gum.

"That was nice of somebody."

"No teacher." He smiled. Last 5.000 dong finish!

We bought our tickets and boarded the boat, glad to be out of harm's way. The ride home was soothing and we talked as much as we could in English and Vietnamese as we made our way back to Haiphong. When we go back to his home, Khanh said, we would all have the shrimp dinner that we had longed for. 'Ahh,' that sounded nice. And Chinh offered to find us some 'home' karaoke at someone's house he knew so we could have an appropriate vacation experience. 'Cool,' said someone to that. And Thanh, for his part, had enjoyed playing soccer on the beach more than he expected and thought that it would be fun to go out and play some more. After we get lunch, though, said Khanh.

"Wait!" I said as we were all disembarking in Haiphong." We were four miles away from home still with exactly zero left. There were no phones in those days. *"How in the world are we going to get home?"*

Toshiba, Inc.

When we came back from our winter conference in Thailand, after the fall of September 11th, 2001, Tet had already come and gone. Not too long had passed since they had repainted the dormitories. Now, we came back to a lot of other new facelifts and makeovers. The season was still cold, and all the Navigation and Economic students had been given these beautiful new blue blazers. They marched together from the dormitory area to the classroom area that I had been taken to on that first day of teaching years ago. As you pass by, they look like West Point Cadets now because the blazers came with very handsome matching white Navy hats with black visors for both boys and girls. In conjunction with these changes, all the classrooms were fitted with shelves in the back of the rooms to place them during class, and all the blackboards had been updated from wooden ones that really belonged in an village in Africa to expensive-looking ones that feel 'oh-so-smooth' when running a piece of chalk down them. It was *months* before anyone wanted to take the plastic off the aluminum frames. New tables, it was told to us, were coming—tables that did not have test answers, names and slightly obscene pictures scrawled all over them.

The very last of the "old rooms" with little iron bars through which so many students had passed cheat-sheets to each other were demolished. Good riddance, we all believed, even though nostalgic, nobody liked the way they caught rain water and thus filled up with mosquitos. All classrooms now were still often exposed to the elements, but at least had elevated concrete floors and doors that closed smoothly.

"We have a new system of naming the classes. I think you will like it." Mrs. Thanh wasn't re-assigning our classes, just going through the big changes with us after another marathon opening ceremony had passed to welcome us all back after Tet. The occasion for all these huge changes was the school's 40 year anniversary. A good impression had brought in much new funding and no expense was being spared to at least make it look as good as its reputation.

"Your foreign trade class will now be called 'KTN-41' and navigation classes will now be 'KTT-39' and '40.' The KTN stands for "Kinh Te Ngoai" (Foreign Trade) and the KTT stands for "Kieu Tien Tau Bien" (Driving Ship). The 40 and 41 stand for how many years ago the school began from the time they began.

"What's wrong with 911 and 921?" I wanted to say, "You mean you have to do math *and* learn Vietnamese to remember it??" Anyway, life never gets simpler as it goes, does it?

So I returned to classes ready to make a difference, with all the new attitudes that hopefully came with new attire, a new set of books bought in Thailand, and now a new name. Everyone had new haircuts from Tet, and according to Vietnamese tradition each person was now a year older, including me. "So, what are we waiting for? Happy New Year. Let's get started, shall we?"

Another new thing for me was the Master's Degree in TESOL and a fundamental change had infected me through it. I genuinely wanted students to do well. The whole career, I had conceded, just like my predecessor Greg had done, just to get by. I still remember him saying (in our original golden conversation), "Yeah, I just pick up a book, glance at it and say, 'yeh. That'll do.' And then go play soccer for hours." Greg's professionalism had grown with his new assignment in a more professional setting. I'd been doing that kind of thing here too, but I wanted to do better, *before* I left for a new assignment. I planned my last few classes around this desire to make a good strong lasting impression if I could.

Not that it had been wrong to match the solution to the task. By the end of the third year and into the last one at Vimaru, I had compiled a 'grab bag' set of favorite lessons that worked. Among these was, oddly enough, the old game show "Jeopardy." We played this often, as it had just about the right amount of prep, took the right amount of time, and could be used to study any set of vocabulary or head-knowledge. The only thing I did away with, except once or twice, was the conversion of answers to questions. It didn't need to be complicated like that. I just wrote both question and answer on a little sheet of paper which I kept in my hand, with the same grid and questions and answers in categories. Then, I wrote the same rows and columns in chalk on the board: across, it said "Kinds of ships," "Verbs," "Participial Clauses," "Students in our class," whatever topic was desired, and beneath each on in columns: "100," "200," "300," "400," and "500." It never got old. We could have played it every day!

"I'll take 'Kinds of ships' for 500." The students never failed to be greedy and go straight for the big dollars. I always wanted to say "No, that's not how you play it! (They never do that on the show!)" but they never listened, and so they always missed the questions, letting someone else grab all the easy points toward the end and win it. "Ok, ok, *have it your way*. Kinds of ships for 500, here we go..."

"What kind of ship passes pulsars and galaxies and has a hyper drive? The Millennium Falcon is one of these." I always made the pricey ones hard like that.

"Uhhh, Lolo wessels teacher?"

"Wrong!!! Anybody else?"

"Cargo ship, teacher."

"Wee-eell, there is that *one* scene..."

"I know, I know! Lash vessel."

"No! It's a *space* ship! Now, who wants to choose the 100 one? Anybody?"

Nobody.

"Hmmm," said the next person in line from the other team, "the only five hundred left is 'verbs?' I'll take it."

"There are so many 300s and 400s to choose from!! But...*have it your way*!" They were playing on teams and I think they thought if they didn't choose the highest number they would let their team down. "What is the third person plural of a synonym for the verb 'utilize?' "

"W--*whhhat*, teacher??"

"Wrong!! Who else wants to fry, from the other team?"

"Do you mean 'try,' teacher?"

"No, I mean 'fry.'

One of the problems with group work was that it always degenerated into chaos. By "group work," I mean two or three people sitting across from each other trying to have a conversation without anybody checking them. By 'chaos,' I mean chaos. Without somebody looking over their shoulders, all but the best students at Vimaru would always almost immediately disengage. They didn't even have phones, and I can't *imagine* what this must be like now! We tried everything, from rearranging the combinations of conversation partners from equal skill-level to completely opposite skill level to random. None of it seemed to work much better than the other, except that when you did opposing skill levels, the good students just complained about the attitudes of the bad ones and if you did equal skill-level, you either had to cut the line free on the lower half and let the unmotivated ones drift off to something else, or you had to babysit them so closely to make them do their work. Although it wasn't easy, I learned to solve this problem through new technology. Well, new to us. Recording.

Technology is such a mixed bag. We now live in an age where even students in Vietnam are completely absorbed and influenced by phones, but it's also an age where recording and turning in work digitally is easy. All we had that could record at that time were little tape players, but they had become cheap and so I could afford a big box of them. Even if one didn't work, the students just had to *think* it worked, as I watched on and made mental notes. We set the cassette players on each table and I crafted the most meticulous test to date. Granted, I was doing it for a class, so it merited more attention, but to this day, test or not, it is one of the activities I am most proud of. Having a recording of each person talking like an ordinary person in a semi-casual "English Club" environment was ingenious, if I don't say so myself!

Real scenarios were created, where each student at each table was assigned a job, simplified down to jobs like 'designer,' 'chairman,' 'financial planner,' etc. They were role playing simple concepts that were accessible—for instance, the 'financial planner' should always make a big deal about money, but the 'visionary' should try to push a better vision, no matter what the cost. Therefore, some realistic conflict could be generated to make things interesting. There were a couple of conversations that were rigidly crafted in advance like this, such as the building of an airport, and topics were also narrowed down for them in the form of problem-solving, such as deciding where should it be built, whether there should there be one big or two small airports, etc. I think the building of a new stadium was another one.

Even with these standards in place, there was room for deviation. Students could receive bonus points, for instance, if they thought of new controversial arguments that weren't on the list but still generated good conversation. Most importantly, though it was a little hard to do, I could pick out who was doing all the talking and give scores based on whether or not you were involved. Because the students are wired and conditioned to be cooperative, not competitive, they often pushed the students with poor English at the table to talk more. It was exactly what they needed. Students who knew English just fine had to use restraint and help the others, not be a showoff. It was exactly what *they* needed.

Other Vietnamese teachers at the school had no problem with English clubs. As long as you do them on your own time. It always felt a little squeamish when one of them walked by my class during these grouping experiments that generated so much indistinguishable noise. Classrooms were open air, and fairly close to one another. The grounds always went from buzzy to eerie quiet when the bell rang. Walking out into the courtyard during session meant that you walked by class after class of silent, regimented students dutifully taking notes (or sleeping) and you could hear the sound of one teacher giving lecture in the same way that you could hear the squeaky spokes of a bicycle out in the countryside in the absence of engines and horns. The minute the bell rang or the first class was released, the air was filled with lots of clamor and noise—making teachers uncomfortable when another teacher lets them out early, like I did that second day of teaching.

We made it a point to visit the other teachers' classes, but it was painful to sit through. We wanted them to know that we wanted to learn from them, and we did. I didn't tell them *what* I wanted to learn, though! For me it was 'what can I get away with and what can't I?" Teachers did sometimes try to be creative. One teacher said "I am going to be creative today," so I wasn't sure what was coming. Her "creativity," it turned out, was to do her lecture on economics with sentences using "Tom & Jerry," as subjects, "Because the students like Tom and Jerry very much," she said. Another teacher did make placards with verb tenses, and when a student answered the question, he or she was allowed to pick another student. As you can see, this is risk-taking of a rather low degree. So whenever a teacher walked by my class down the silent row and peered in to see all the students shouting at each other as if it were the school cafeteria, I wondered if this class might be my last. Occasionally, a teacher would walk by inquisitively to see what was the matter, and whether or not any at all teacher was even in the classroom. Seeing me, they would be a tad startled, but walk away just shaking their head. "What do these foreign teachers know about teaching, anyway?" I hoped they weren't thinking it, but I'm sure some of them were.

I took comfort that what we did worked. Students were becoming better, at least I felt. It wasn't completely to our credit—they had been drilled to death by other teachers and just needed to use what they already knew. I could tell the acquisition of better English was much due to these teachers by those 'perfect imperfections,' the way all the students made the same errors with confidence meant that they had been taught consistently and well by somebody. At this time, almost all of them (they told me often) had only learned Russian as kids. I also learned to see myself and others as having a different role than the Vietnamese English teachers—I just hoped they'd understand it the same way.

I might not have tried this had it not been toward the end of the year, or if the career here wasn't toward the end and the contract considered not to be renewed with Vimaru for that matter. But I learned through one spring activity this year that we teachers did not hold the market on creativity. I decided to go 'no-holds-barred' again and this time divided (well, I had done it already in the fall) all my students into permanent groups—this time I called them companies. Since these were foreign trade students this time, a co-ed class who were going to use their English in the marketplace, we made it as real as possible, forgoing the cute "sea-dogs," "octopus" titles from before and making them actual companies. They were real ones, such as "Toshiba," "Dilmah Tea," "Daihatsu," and other big companies known to the students. I even had them elect a president who served as a kind of mini-monitor for each group. With this structure in place, I was able to hand them a blank check for their presentations.

"All you have to do for the rest of the class, besides the book and regular exam you have to take of course, is to present your company to the rest of the group, in English of course. At the end, everybody will have a certain amount of money to buy stock in your companies, and whoever sells the most stock wins. That's it." In the back of my mind, I almost totally expected it to be a disaster. "They won't come up with anything," I thought.

Boy was I wrong.

After a few weeks of doing drills and games in class and having no idea what was going on behind closed dorm-doors, the first group, Dilmah Tea, was given their chance to present their product to everybody in the class. Thankfully, they had a cheap enough product, and someone had decided to take advantage of that by throwing paper table-cloths over the table and coming in with buckets of watered down...Dilmah tea. A man with a real fake mustache got up in front of the class and gave a spiel, like a used-car-salesman, why you should buy Dilmah not Lipton, and they had people go around and do a taste-test. The presentation was wonderful, and I told them afterwards.

"Pretty good! If the rest of you do something like that, you'll all do very well." In the back of my mind, though, I was worried. The volume level of our class had intensified. Students loved the "small party" idea, but parties in Vietnam are not exactly quiet. If a regular group conversation activity was at a decibel of 3 out of ten (1 being all the other classes), this was a 5. Someone had even brought in a guitar and sang a jingle that had been written for the occasion. It was followed by lots of whooping and clapping and "do it again!!" *Dilmah* had set a pretty stinkin' high standard. But this is just the first day. I had never tested a fragile system like this before, we had ten presentations left for the next ten days!

Day four...thankfully days two and three had been relatively tame. This time, one of my students Duc, (Pham Minh Duc) broke the creativity barrier with his rendition of...me.

I had never been parodied before, and his representation was a hoot. He had on a backward baseball hat, just so everybody would 'get it,' and otherwise his regular uniform with a tie. He started off class exactly like I always do, by calling roll call, intentionally not using tones, dropping middle names or leaving out names altogether. The bottom had fallen out of the class—they were all laughing. Duc ran to the back of the room and grabbed this one girl's hands and then violently dragged her up to the front (do I do that??) and then mercilessly proceeded to interrogate her with hard and funny questions like "what is a *chemistry set*?" Then he would start making people leave by force for doing silly things and he hadn't even given an exam yet. Students and I were rolling on the floor with tears on our faces.

When he gave the exam, Duc grabbed a big stack of papers and smashed them down in front of everyone and then hovered like hawks the way Manny and I do, putting his face up inches away from theirs one-by-one in an exaggerated way. Apparently Vietnamese teachers aren't so meticulous.

Then he started to throw candy at them, which I must have done before at some point, though I have tried not to do that ever since I read a study my friend Greg had shared with us. The "Lame Duc" was so entertaining that I wanted to give him an "A" on the spot, but the presentation had to be combined with a lackluster report by everybody else in the group to pass muster and actually advertise *Nippon Steel*, which admittedly did not have a whole lot to do with teaching or me.

The next day, I knew something strange was up because calling roll revealed to me that the absentees matched Toshiba company, which was due to do their presentation that day. I stuck my head out just to see and... oh...my...g,g,g,g,

A large Disney character was walking our way.

"Holy emojis Batman!" I thought, "Let's get this mayhem out of bedlam!!" I signaled to hurry up and not stall.

I knew this creature as the big blue Japanese cat that is on all the milk cartons, but I think its name is Doreamon. The whole idea was to make this grand entrance and surprise everybody but Toshiba had gotten into a squall with the guards at the front gate who weren't going to let them in with that thing on. When they finally managed, it was five minutes into classroom time, so our Disney parade caught the attention of every single other classroom, since our room was conveniently situated at the back of the school. I had once thought of this as fortunate. They had gone out and rented a couple of big fancy costumes, and I think we can safely call this a "first" for the school. Quite a few other teachers and students had gathered for this unexpected and rather interesting even but embarrassingly, the big head got stuck in the doorway which was a wee bit small, and the mysterious cat character had to pop his head out to be just Kien.

"Hi Kien."

"Hi, teacher."

Somebody finally hammered the head all the way in and Kien turned back into the cat, which was then pushed around in a kind of morality play that may or may not sell Toshiba computers. The other teachers were really scratching their heads now about us, if they had not been doing so when we simply had tea talk, and I was like, about to call an emergency press conference right on the spot, except I could tell that some of the teachers kind of liked it and were dancing a little bit with the Japanese Cat. One thing was sure, nobody was going to miss my class tomorrow, and I don't mean just my students.

Thankfully, we were near the end, but unthankfully, one of the last groups decided to go big or go home with some kind of military drama and people dressed like people on the political posters. I buried my head as deep in my hands as they go, wondering if I might end up in some kind of gulag for teaching counter-cultural heresies. At least they left Ho out of it, but who around here has ever heard of using soldiers, sailors and revolutionary factory workers to sell Dove soap? The military marching sounds emanating from the classroom is about as natural of a sound as the birds and honking in this place, but I could still remember the old admonition "Teach them ONLY English!" When the other teachers realized there was no dancing cat this time but just the same ol' ho-hum propaganda, they were like, "Oh well, party's over, I guess" and went back to their own teaching.

We ended the semester just like any other, with those dull (and terrifying) final exams at tables with the other teachers. But I think the creative projects did something special. They made this class bond and grow comfortable in English. Though everyone would disperse soon after and perhaps not do so well on the official interrogation tests, they came over to my room more often as a friend and that, more than anything, is probably what did it. Later, I came up with the great idea to make beautiful portrait photography of each student and had fun doing this. Students didn't want the fun to end and begged and pleaded for a separate English Club with the little time we had left to keep doing fun stuff like this. Though I wouldn't expect the Vietnamese teachers to go as crazy as I had in their classes, I would imagine that they may have moved an inch or two closer to fun that day. And in Vietnamese culture, that's a mile...or a Kilometer, I should say.

Jingle (Mission) Bells

Manny's favorite time of year was not Christmas day. It was a day or two prior to that when he put his little pinky toe over the line and shared the (Christian) bridge illustration with his students. He did the whole thing too, the perfectly drawn cross he'd been practicing all year with the chasm of death, and by walking across, salvation is the greatest gift that can be given to any person.

"I just do it year after year, and hope that somehow, something will sink in. The Holy Spirit works all year, but we are teachers under contract, so I can do this sort of thing only at Christmas."

Though I didn't do this exact talk with my students, I did similar things. We all did. We were walking the line between our contracts and a higher mandate. Even for those who are not inclined toward faith, it would be hard to keep such out of a conversation on Western culture. Information is only one tiny catalyst, and we prayed for our students all day and sipped tea with them all night, and kept in mind all the appropriate 'legal' channels to share our lives with these student in hopes that something would be noticed. But Christmas seemed to be this free-for-all time that came once a year. It is one of Vietnam's four 'official' religious holidays, the other three being Buddhist.

"Today, we will play Christmas Jeopardy. So who will go first?"

"Teacher, when we have exams?"

"Um. Next time. Shall I call roll now? We have a story about that. Old man winter—that's what they call Santa Claus—he keeps a list of who is naughty and nice." I couldn't resist.

"Teacher, does Old Man Winter deliver packages to ships on the sea?" Nobody ever asked that, but I always thought that would be the best question.

"Teacher," pointing to another boy, "He is *boofallo*." Everybody laughs.

"He is *monkey*!!"

Oh brother. "So, shall I mark you all naughty then?"

"Teacher, will you go to church on Christmas?"

She means Christmas Eve. In Vietnam there is not Christmas day; maybe for a few Christians who relish this holiday like it is a second Tet. But for everyone else, Christmas consists of one visit to the church. You may remember that, though I don't know it's coming in this scene, this is where I lost my wallet there. I had to wait all night to get my bicycle back because the little ticket was inside. But, I digress.

"Yes, we are! I'm sure it will be fun. We'll take bikes."

"Teacher, who is the baby?"

Every so often, a miraculous question like this would drop out of the sky out of nowhere. The baby! Yes, I thought you'd never ask. That is the original Christmas story. I'll give you a preview, but if you really want to live it up, you absolutely must come to the ultimate Christmas party at my house.

Safely out of the watchful eye of our big brothers and sisters in the animal farm, we had our own manger scene at my house. Donna Summer may have played a part in it, as well as "Michael Learns to Rock." Three perfect tinfoil crowns sat waiting by an angelic costume of sparkley Christmas tree snake ornaments and lights adorning our angels. These students didn't know they were going to become actors. We had them come in to the disco scene with the kind of high energy expected for a Christmas party. We didn't want anyone reporting a church service at our house after all.

"Merry Chwistmass, teacher we buy you gift!"

"Oh, you aren't supposed to do that! That's teacher's day. This is students' day. Have some chocolates." We broke our rules about giving amazing imports to students. They were so hard to acquire and nobody ever liked them as much as the red pumpkin seeds that were practically free, but we made the sacrifice. Of course, we were often rolling in Christmas memorabilia, having received some in care packages and others acquired simply because the things purchased here were so quaint and exciting.

We've got music—the best Christmas disco. We'll start with the Back Street Boy's playing "Mary's Boy Child." It wasn't really the Back Street Boys, but this song had been covered by every band in Vietnam. It was the absolute hit at the time, which struck us all as strangely (and conveniently) counter-cultural.

"I wanted to make sure you practiced the English to *Mary's Boy Child*, so I made you all copies of the words!" If you don't know the song, there is a highly evangelistic message and nobody can call this propaganda if it made it past the Communist censors when even M.C. Hammer couldn't.

"Ok, after we listen to Marys Boy Child, can we all sing *25 Minutes*?"

"Um. Ok." Trying to think if that song had any redemptive content.

I liked our Christmas parties because they seemed to incorporate everything right about evangelism here. They were sanctioned, at least faintly, and no less appropriate than a Teacher's Day visit. We did the parties as a community and if we had enough interested students we could do it several times for each others' whole sets of friends. We could be pretty direct about the incarnation—it's at the core of the Christian message and a major fork in the road from Buddhism, but it's not so offensive because there are enough Catholics here to give it some validity. Everybody went on a romantic date to look at the weird life-sized nativities that were totally unpredictable and yet, they all at least had the baby that was asked about. Here, we could like our pageants to the famous iconography and fill in the details. And add the secret ingredient to any successful communication here—music—and you have a message.

It was easy to overdo it. Maybe that's why I have a funny memory of what felt like an out of control teenage sleepover at a Hanoi pageant once. Again, I don't remember what year it was, but the whole thing was done with a pile of sheets and blankets. Thankfully, though, there wasn't a huge need for props because by that time, the Schallers and others involved had good enough language to make it interesting.

"And then, Mary was pregnant. Somebody grab me wonna those pillows! Here, put this under your jacket, you can be Mary. Now...we need someone to be a don-key..."

Why didn't I think of that?'

"So, Mary had to go on... the DONKEY," everybody is laughing at this point.

"Wait..., *what's that sound*?" It was not part of the show.

"Aaaagh! He's going over the fence!!" Yes, somebody had grabbed one of the girls' bicycles, right as the shepherds were donning their plaid flannel cloaks.

"Grab him!!!!" But it was too late. He had tossed the bike over and hopped over himself, and was already mounted by the time we figured out how to unlock the gate.

"Oh *bummer*! How can we finish our story *now*?" sighed David.

"It's ok." Said the girl whose bike was stolen. She was trying to suppress tears.

"Well, let's *see*. Hmmm. Shepherds? How can we make this relevant?"

David gave it a good shot. The shepherds left their bikes with the sheep and were so overjoyed that when they came back, they didn't care anymore. But it didn't work. We spent the rest of the night trying to figure out what had happened and how to buy the girl another bike without it being weird.

So, my night went quite a bit better.

"Here Khanh," this was the time we did his class, the original 711 which may have been the best memory of these. "You get to be king."

"Ah! I like king."

"But you haven't heard the story yet. King Herod is bad...very bad. He killed a bunch of babies. But never mind, you are one of the *good* kings."

"You mean me and two others?" I must have told him the story before.

"Right. Uh, ...Yes! Pick two others. I don't care. Here I have two more crowns." So we had three kings, some shepherds, and the angels of course we had to do up ridiculous. In this class of boys, it was a little tricky to find a Maria (as they used the Catholic name). And I had to explain that Old Man Winter wasn't part of the story, but Manny ruined it when he came out with his Santa hat anyway.

"Ho ho ho,"

"Wait Manny, *what are you doing?* We're still doing the nativity scene!"

"Oh,... sorry."

"Here is the king I was talking about!!," (*psst. Manny! Be Herod. You're Herod!*) I had to salvage this somehow. What better way to restore Christmas than to make Old Man Winter Herod? I was far too preoccupied to notice my own brilliance in the moment.

"Who will be the babies?"

"No!!! Come on!! We don't have babies. Oh, well, here's the baby Jesus doll. Wait, I'm getting ahead of things. Here Mary, I mean...Maria...put this under your shirt. Be gentle!"

"Ok, now where were we." I had rigged for Brian to surprise us and bring trays of cakes and cookies just as we were all huddled in awe and coddling the baby Jesus, but I wasn't hearing anything. My voice grew gradually louder as the time grew nearer.

"*Ahem,* sooo, MARRRIIIAAA then began to have the baby. (nudge-nudge)."

"Aughg!!!" screamed Mr. Maria in his best lady's voice.

Do it a little louder. Where *is* he?

"AAAUUUGHTHGHT!!" I heard scrambling in the kitchen.

"Oh, good good! Now... *ahem* SHEPHERDS CAME INTO THE BARN." I urged the animal choir to go crazy.

"Buffalo and monkey, *especially* you two!" the self-casted actors were beyond perfect, of course.

FINALLY the tray. Where were you?

"Sorry, I had students in the hallway."

"Oh well, never mind. Wait, I should try to get to the evangelistic part before we dive into cookies, huh?"

"Ok, we'll do it together."

"Why don't you let Manny do it? He's got the Santa hat."

"No, you missed that part, he's Herod." Our teamwork wasn't always up to par, I'll admit.

"Soo! People. Let me tell you the story first again. JESUS is the baby. He was the great God who came to the earth as a little baby so he could grow up to be...wait a minute. I have a better idea. Where are those song lyrics? Now..., when the shepherds and Maria and Josep and monkey and buffalo were gathered together. They all had a song. Are you ready, we are going to sing it!

Long time ago in Bethlehem, so the Holy Bible said,
Mary's boy child Jesus Christ, was born on Christmas Day.

Hark, now hear the angels sing, a king was born today,
And man will live for evermore, because of Christmas Day.
Mary's boy child Jesus Christ, was born on Christmas Day.

While shepherds watch their flocks by night,
    (and buffalo and monkey too*)
they see a bright new shining star,
they hear a choir sing a song, the music seemed to come from afar.

Hark, now hear the angels sing, a king was born today,
And man will live for evermore, because of Christmas Day.

That's what I was trying to say! If you believe in Jesus, you will too live forevermore. All because of Christmas day! So, um. Then, there were all these angels from heaven who were singing—actually that was out in the field...wait, *I'm doing this out of order, aren't I?*"

"What about me?" asked the king.

"Hold on. So, um...there were angels who already met the shepherds once, and this isn't in the Holy Bible, but they have cookies."

"No wait. Maybe this works better. Give the cookies to the kings."

"Yes, we are kings of orient are." (So he knew that one too.)

"I *know*, but they aren't for *you*. They are for the baby. See? You present them to the baby Jesus, and ...if we follow Jesus, then he gives us cookies!" I was now venturing into the health-and-wealth theology zone, wasn't I?

"And *we give our cookies to each other*!! See how it works?"

Anyways. Our magic moment was pretty much fleeting at this point.

Our contextualized performances were only one slice of the Christmas pie, of course. We generally did everything we could think to do. Apart from our own family activities, which I've already alluded to, we had our house done up well and we gave hints to the other teachers at the school to come and visit. When they came, I had the "wonderful counsellor" verse huge on the wall, and all of Manny's Christmas cards. That's another thing. They looovveeedd Christmas cards, so what we did, and Manny did it best, was tell people to send their old Christmas cards from years before instead of throwing them away and we had literally piles of them. By cutting off the back sometimes, or just leaving them be, we could give them out to everyone. Manny would write these wonderful notes in them, while I chose the ones that were more pre-loved. One of the things we sometimes chuckled at was that Christmas lights here are really "Tet" lights. Only the hokey portraits of Santa are seen genuinely as Christmas, or the nativity or Santa. Even the nativity could veer a little into weirdness, because everything at Catholic churches was statues, statues, statures. And holy items that sold for a premium. The Christmas pictures were just knockoffs of the more popular pictures of Buddha, and Santa was just—ridiculous. I even saw him once directing traffic.

We had a mouse-sized Christmas tree and made some dummy presents to complement the few that we had rewrapped (as you may recall, the Post Office had to see what everything was). Presents were the other things that characterized Christmas, and my secular intellectual friend Quan never grew tired of telling us that Christmas is really more of a Vietnamese holiday than an American one, because they are atheists. It always made me mad, because I knew he kind of had a point about that, the way it is celebrated. In Vietnam, the more contemporary culture changed the words metaphorically to be "Hark the diamond, Macy's sings!" It had become sort of what Valentine 's Day was supposed to be. Quan told us that Vietnamese think mostly of their girlfriend when Christmas comes. With all this tackiness and distraction, it was hard to know how to restore dignity, but we knew that no matter how bad it was, it was still pretty pure here. Everyone knew that this is the Christian's big day, and they seemed to do Christmas so much better than American Christians do. For everyone outside those circles, it was a void that had to be filled by something. I think it was hard for the teachers to miss that we had some fondness for something to do with Christmas.

One time, I even invited Khanh's whole family over. It was so awkward, because I'd never seen them out of their own home, and they were trying to figure out how to behave here like I always was there. I just had snacks—at that point I completely chickened out on doing a whole meal—but I did gradually learn how to use Vietnamese to give a much less zany, more direct presentation. I remember them leaving thinking that it had all been very nice—and clear, though I hoped that Khanh's report of the previous party did not lead them to think somehow that the Bible contradicts itself!

The Language Centre

My reason for residence in Hanoi in 2003 was not to teach, but to study Vietnamese. I was enrolled in my company's program at a small school. The focus was continued one-on-one study, as we had been doing, rather than classroom instruction. The head of the school, Mr. Thai, was nice enough, but our school was located one building over from the School of Internal Affairs, where students learned who would read our mail and listen in on our phones—and it showed. The schoolmaster always had a distance in his eyes that made us nervous, even if we had nothing illegal that we were doing to be caught for.

Into this environment, I began to study—or I should say, continued to study—Vietnamese. My actual teacher, named Thao, was a pleasant agreeable lady about the age of my mom who liked to smile and when she corrected, did so with an apology. We were ploughing, and I mean really ploughing through an improved biography of my life at the beginning, which I had constructed roughly and wanted to improve.

"So far, I've perfected the story of my first memory, and the chapters on Disney World and my love of Star Wars. I'm so glad to know the word for "stormtrooper" and "jedi" (which disappointingly is 'je-di'). Today, I need help with a new episode."

Now, my dear reader, I am translating to English for you, because by this time, thankfully, I was able to struggle through entire sessions in Vietnamese.

"You have a story here about losing your tooth?" asked Thao.

"That's right. But not the first time. Not the *baby* tooth. I lost a *permanent* tooth when I was nine."

"Well,... this should be good then."

"It's another bicycle fail. I think this is why I'm scared of the road."

Mrs. Thao didn't know she would be doing therapy sessions too. "I see you already have made many mistakes." She says this in English.

"Correct me please!"

So, we corrected the passage until it looked like the following (I leave the tones out):

"*Mot ngay khac, to muon em trai va toi dap thi nhau. Em trai dong y voi hai be trai khac va chung toi bat dau day nhung chiec xe cua chung toi len doi. Dong nguy hiem qua vi vay chung toi dinh di tren le dong nhung no rat hep va khong co du choc ho hai xe dap. Khi toi co gang di qua xe dap cua em nhang nhung chop thi can phai di tren co gho ghe. To bi nga manh va moi ngoui lien dung lai. Toi da mat mot rang va cam thay rat dau, dac biet khi toi ngam mieng. Toi phai di nha si voi cai mieng mo. Toi nho toi da nghi rang chiec rang moi cua toi xau lam boi vi mau hoi khac. Toi hy vong khong bao gio xay ra nua.*"

Basically, I had written the following English sentence:

"Another day, I wanted my brother and I to ride side by side on our bikes. My brother agreed, and we started racing fast down a sidewalk. The way was so dangerous because the two of us wanted to go around each other on a narrow path and didn't really have enough space to pass each other. When I tried to do just that, my bike tripped over his and I hit the hard, rough pavement. I felt a hard thrusting pain and everyone stopped in the path. I had lost a tooth, and felt much pain, especially when I closed my mouth. So I had to go to the dentist with my mouth open. No when I think back, I realize how ugly I felt to have to endure it and I hope it never happens again."

Our learning of Vietnamese was almost a hundred percent directed by us, which had huge advantages and naturally some blind spots. When I moved on to Cambodia and worked on that language, I learned to appreciate classroom learning in its own right, but we had been given some excellent training and of course, had practiced training our own teachers over the years.

"Now, is it ok if we go through these flash cards I prepared?"

I had spent quite a bit of time learning a process called today *The Growing Participators' Approach* by linguist Greg Tompson, who worked for SIL and who I considered my best distance mentor. I never met him, though he did workshops in places like Hanoi, but I devoured his theoretical material and used it to make my own lessons. They used a lot of props like toy cars, dolls and things around the house, as well as pictures. I had fond memories of training my friend Tran Khanh, whose face would light up after about an hour of bossing me around in Vietnamese and making me do stuff he said; and then he would say, "Wait a minute, this works doesn't it? Do me in English then!!" So I would boss him around and he would learn.

"Now, child. This is not effective," said Mrs. Thao.

So often we had to have these talks before we used the flash cards.

"I know. I just want to do it so I have the words on tape."

Something like that usually worked as an explanation. Recording the lesson once meant I could do it several more times, although it was often extraordinary if I could find time to sit down and do it even once before the next wave of material came crashing into my schedule.

"You want to do it again??"

"Just one more time, Mrs. Thao, then we can go on break."

The Hanoi Language Center had an ordinary sounding name, but Mark had sought it out precisely because this laid-back approach made it perfect for using our materials, such as the "growing participator approach" which is an early pre-cursor to the now wildly popular Rosetta Stone software. The process is to Rosetta Stone what an abacus is to a calculator, but somehow preparing the lesson ourselves gave us insight into the 'why' of the process in the same way that building a car would be more helpful than buying one for understanding potential breakdowns.

It was also close to our home, which meant that our world was intimate and local. I lived with Peter Galbraith, who also studied at the same school, along with Art Carter and Sherman Chau. Sherman was the only one of us who was married, and he lived with his wife Becky in a villa close to ours. The house occupied by Peter and I was the original house that had been the home of (surfer-dude) Chad Wilshire from the beginning. Because of that, I had memories that were stacked as high as the five-storied tube-building that towered high indeed because each room had twelve-foot ceilings.

Houses in Hanoi always go up, because once-upon-a-time during land reforms, each family was given a modest twelve-foot-wide home that goes deep like a pringles' can, about forty-five feet in. When some households became richer than others—a trend that isn't supposed to happen too much in Communist planning—they shot up to the heavens, while others eeked out an extra loft or two, giving the neighborhood a fairly jagged local skyline. From the street though, every house looked pretty much the same if you didn't crane your neck. Our house was not ornate by any stretch, and once inside, the bare-chested bachelor-pad became apparent. Colors didn't match too well, and whatever could be scrounged up was slapped on the walls, but we loved the place. It worked for us.

Sandy's cute neighborhood was a quadrant or two over, and the team of teachers at the Foreign Trade School was about that far in another direction making the teacher triangle. All of us were away from the part of town where tourists go—the Hoan Kiem Lake and the Old Quarter. That is how we wanted it to be. The panhandlers didn't know about us. The motorcycle taxi men didn't know any better to charge us. And most importantly, the restaurants didn't cater to us—just let us into the regular scenes, where we could have plenty of affordable food and great conversations with almost any customer in the joint we chose, and with each other.

"Anh em se noi chuyen ve gi ha anh?" I asked Peter in butchered Vietnamese. In fact, I'll translate it the way a Vietnamese lunch-goer at our table would have overheard us.

"What we should be practice on my dear brother?" Vietnamese no easy, I make bad today. Why you bad today make, brother? Me teacher do me exercise bicycle going turn turn back, *I mean* bicycle turning match exercise. Oh weekly back I turn turn exercise me too (indistinguishable word). When I did study bicycle my lesson today me history go go to write back again by Vietnamese. Ahh...I understand you clearly, brother. So, do you everly write back your story by Vietnamese no? I no. I eat now, you need eat by chopsticks my dear brother, or the spoon use?"

We tried not to think about what we sounded like, Peter and I in the café. I think both of us were trying to impress each other, but it was a great regular discipline because we did know some different words. But nothing turns lunchtime joy to drudgery like forcing yourself to think while you dine when your eggs are already fried. We sometimes left feeling better about our own Vietnamese though, because somehow—far from impressing each other—we only impressed ourselves because we only knew the mistakes made by the other. But our table mates must have certainly had the last laugh!

Though it has been lost, I still have a photocopy of a priceless document from this period. It is the complete blueprint of the first half of my semester—a grail diary with the path to fluency. It is a true gem because I took the time to re-write the words carefully from sloppier notes made in class, and to carefully document the nine assignments I had given myself to last the semester. Hard, I made them. Ambitious, I was.

In Vietnam, the Mekong River splits into nine canals and nine is generally an auspicious number. That is the only reason I can think of for not doing ten, other than the notion that nine just about killed me. Going into the spring, I had sketched these out in conjunction with the brand new tan language books that had just been released by the Foreign Language University of Vietnam. I was interested in immersion and kicking my own butt with these, but I also wanted to involve Art and Peter and Sherman. So, to kick us off, I list the first four. (1.) Make Five Telephone Calls in Vietnamese, (2.) Visit a Vietnamese Family, (3.) Host a Vietnamese Party, (4.) Interview Four People in the Community, doesn't sound so bad, does it?

*Ring, Rrrrriinnnnnnggg!**

In these days, we still used the old plastic corded-wall telephones.

"Hello?" said Sherman.

"Alo."

"Oh come on. Are you kidding me?? *hm* I mean, 'Oi gioi anh Hayden, anh co van de hay em co gang lam bai tap voi em ha??"

This was just a practice call, though I did use Peter as one of my four. Calling was just so dang intimidating! Had I known that people in the future would text, I might have tossed this whole endeavor as a useless skill, but nothing tests your language like stripping all the visual cues away with most of the non-verbal communication.

*Ring, Rrrrriinnnnnnggg!**

"Alo."

"(In well-rehearsed Vietnamese) Hello, I am American Vietnamese. I have come to invest in Vietnam because in my country, there is a stigma against Vietnamese and I want to bring good message to my country."

"I'm sorry, is this..."

"No! No joke. I have money. I run a restaurant here in Hanoi and I need to find a local studio to film a commercial. See, I like to do kung fu. Like Vietnamese see?"

click...

I looked into the receiver.

"Well, I guess prank calls are for advanced students only," I sighed to Peter beside me.

"There is *no way* that is counting," says Peter as he casually sips his homemade slightly fermented kumquat syrup drink.

I thought it would be funny to recreate a famous Lance Krall comedy sketch from Southern California, but ended up making two very routine calls to my friends' moms, to move me on to where I need to be. However, it was karma that kept me accountable for the first 'cut corner' of this whole enterprise because I did end up making another call in Vietnamese that I had not anticipated—to make up for the lame Sherman call that nobody thought should count. And it happened after I was well into the second of the nine trials.

Having completed the four phone calls to my satisfaction, I moved on to the second trial, which was to visit a friend's home and speak Vietnamese the whole time.

I thought this one should be easy enough. I'd done it many times before. The difference was that I intended to make this one more of a scientific data-clincher. I didn't know too many people in Hanoi, without students, but I did have one friend that I did not tell you about. Paging back to the trip to Cao Bang from the year before, there was another boy named Khanh who I had met on the bus coming home. He'd briefly taken me to his home with an open invite to hook up for a meal or something—any time! It was a perfect setting for a visit to tick the box.

There are a few moments in all my years in Vietnam that strike me as purely magic. It's as if I stepped into a National Geographic Photograph—which is precisely what this one was. Hearkening back (or a year forward from that time) to the year 2004, on page 94 of the May issue, you can take in in the pulsating green fluorescent room with brown-tiled floors and humans huddled against mint-green walls. Only in our case, we were at an all-male meal with rice-wine thimbles that I had once again successfully negotiated out of in Vietnamese. I was spending the weekend at Hanoi-Khanh's home, and we had plans to visit the temple of literature in the morning. The mood of twilight was coming on at that hour when a dangling lightbulb from a seller right outside the window doesn't pierce the eyes, but gives a warm highlight to the cool blue air that signals the final moments of daylight.

Of course, I had a notebook handy, because I wanted to satisfy the second assignment—a visit to a home. "They were so happy I was coming that they bought a pretty big hue flower," I later wrote in both languages. "When I arrived, I didn't bring them a typical gift because I had the notebook for them to read with the stories about me. Hanoi-Khanh's cousin introduced himself as Thang, and of course, when I arrived, it was as if they had been waiting and the food was ready. They weren't in a hurry though, being plenty satisfied with beer. "We've been eager to see you," they said, and that's all I understood for the next two or three minutes. I do know though that much of it had to do with the soccer match that was happening that night and how much money might be lost. I heard plenty of numbers. I tried my best to push the conversation to interesting topics, like the clothes people wear at home and why there might be such an interest in a movie with a black man and a Chinese man partnering in a crime investigation. They eventually ran out of things to ask about, and sent me to bed until the match would begin in the wee hours of the morning, but when I opened my eyes, the room was filled with sunlight. Well, so much for soccer then."

Oh yes. The call. So, after breakfast, the other kid Khanh's mother brings out candy which looks like caramel taffy. They are really proud of it, but as I start to bite into it, I realize that it is like a piece of wood. It's so hard. I start to gnaw on it until I can bite off a bit. Mmmmm. Good! I smile.

The moment needed no words as there were four faces staring at me. They were discerning whether or not I liked the candy. Three of them belonged to the people in the room, and one was from a mirror mounted on the old wooden armoire adjacent to me. Only the effigy of my face had a missing tooth.

My smile died as I pursed my lips together and nearly croaked. I smiled again. "Yikes!!!" I said. This time I jumped back.

"What?" They said.

Never imagining my lesson with Thao would ever be used, about the broken tooth, I said "What do you mean 'what?' My tooth!!"

"Oh...yeah. You're right. *heh*"

"Oh let me brush that bread crumb off your face." That's the kind of tone they were using as if people lost teeth all the time here when they ate the candy.

"I twink I weed to wake a pone caw." I said in English.

Well, that was a nightmare. Thankfully the tooth broke off without opening the nerve, so I felt no pain. I managed to call the clinic they suggested in Vietnamese since I had absolutely no numbers for Peter or anyone, and there was not a good way to just look up 'English dentist' on the yellow pages. The Vietnamese dentist place said they were full, so I finally said "forget it, I'll just do this day as planned and get some good help, since it doesn't hurt." At least I had a legitimate call now logged away to replace the Sherman one. My perfectly planned two-day Vietnamese language lesson was decidedly interrupted though, as we went to the temple of literature and I kept looking for shiny rocks, lakes and spears to keep deciding if my reflection was ugly or not. "Relax!!" said Khanh. "Everybody has broken teeth in Vietnam." Now I knew how everybody feels.

When I finally made a dental appointment with an international English-speaking clinic (no, I am not THAT die-hard of a language learner, but *wouldn't it have made a great expansion* to my home visit!) I came ten minutes late and they were like "You failed!! You can *never* reschedule!"

"But I got stuck in traffic! You know how it is. There are like, thousands and thousands of motorbikes out that door. You can't move an inch on the road." I was telling the truth, but *that was that* and I had to find another clinic. The second clinic had a wonderful foreign dentist named Andrew who gave me a beautiful new white tooth, putting me right back on track for assignment number three!

"Number Three. Host a Vietnamese Party." When I made these, I was thinking of my life in Haiphong, but now that I was here in Hanoi, I was wondering who would come to my party. I could document all the fixins' but for guests??...well, I just didn't have many friends here yet. Maybe that was kind of the point.

"So, who would want to help me make a party to invite some friends to? One of the other teachers, right?"

"Now, you're thinking! How about Kim? She loves to party." Kim was a second or third year teacher at the Foreign Trade University near us.

"Sounds good to me," said Kim on the phone. I'm meeting some people this weekend for a party anyway. "Great."

I hadn't put too much thought or preparation into this one. I just said I needed to have a party for an assignment. Kim just said to grab some balloons and cake and festive ornaments, whatever. By this time, it had already become early April.

So, I meet Kim and she's like, "Hey, it's over at one of their dorms." So when we come up to their dorm, it started raining.

WHHHOOOOOSSSSSHHHHH. A little rain cloud directly over my head, or rather—a bucket.

"My recorder. Drats. I think it's ok. Let me think of some Vietnamese to say—*aauururururrrgghhh*!!"

Hahaha, a bunch of kids came out. I started talking Vietnamese to them, if I could. I would just remember what they say and write it out later, since my notebook was in danger with all this water.

"Choom ripe suueya"

"Kim! *These aren't Vietnamese people.*"

"Oh, you needed Vietnamese people? These are Laotian. Don't you know Laotian New Year? Water Festival? Hel-loooo!"

"No, I need notes for my Vietnamese!!"

"They speak Vietnamese. They're students too. Language students. Ask them something."

"I think they're more interested just in having fun." WHHHOOOOSSSHHH.

Kim and I paid the price of just standing there like ducks.

"Well, you wanted a party. Let's daannnccee!!" Whoop whoop, everybody starts dancing and I'm thinking I might as well start dancing to celebrate the new recording device I'm going to have to buy after this!

Language Task Four: Interview Three People in your immediate community. After interviewing the coffeeshop lady and the one on the corner to makes "banh thit nuong," I asked Peter "who should I interview for my third one? I wonder what would happen if I interviewed Thu."

Thu was Peter's language teacher. She was a character who always made a big deal about her Christian faith. In fact, there was kind of a running debate about whether she was a spy put there by director Thai to peg us once and for all. Or not.

"Come on, I'm sure she's fine," said Mark our language and culture director. He was in favor of giving her the benefit of the doubt. Sure enough, the previous Christmas, Peter had gone to church to look over his shoulder to see her singing her heart out in church.

"I'm not so sure," said David, another leader who advised against telling her anything that might rock the boat.

Peter sat down with her for lessons and found her always engaging. Her charm, for one thing, put her into question.

"Hehe, this is like a Bible study!" she said gleefully. "Wouldn't you like to study the Bible in Vietnamese?"

"No, really, I think we should just stick to the textbook."

"Well, fine then. What's your favorite Bible verse?"

Peter just grimaced, "All's fair in love and war."

"I don't know that one. We Vietnamese have such a proverb though."

"I don't really think you'd find out much," said Peter. "I wouldn't go near her with a ten-foot pole if I were you."

"But I might be of service to figure out who she really is, and knock out my assignment!"

She had been particularly playful and tried to get Peter to give his testimony.

"What did you tell her?"

"That I passed my testimony with flying colors. What about interviewing the film developer? You can talk about all your latest pictures when you pick them up." That's a great idea, I said.

So I did that instead, prolonging my stay in Vietnam by another year.

We are Millionaires Already

Imagine you have been waiting a month to have students, and then your student list looks also a little bit like "less is more." We had hoped that on coming back, our lists would be more full of names.

"Is this really all you think we're going to have this time?" I asked Rich, my new teammate in a new city, Thai Nguyen, which was about forty miles north of Hanoi.

"Yous got even more than I do, look here will ya?," says Rich, who is from West Monroe, Louisiana, as he shows me his list of fourteen. Mine had about twenty.

"We should be thankful. I used to have to remember a hundred names. But even though my list says I have twenty students in one class and fifteen in another, only five showed up. And then only seven. I wonder who these other twenty-three are."

Soon enough, with one year instead of four, I realized I had to be intentional to be influential. A year sounds like a lot of time, but it's actually only nine months, no make that eight if we're going to Thailand and travelling after that. Eight months. No, make that seven if they start a month late. Even with some Vietnamese language, how do you get to know these students well in just seven months? The English language is a relational kind of science, we have to what we called 'lower the affect' to get past the anxiety of being cast into another way of thinking so they can really learn. Out of seven good months, we were already on month four. There is not much time left.

I had only three strategies for out-of-class friendship—visits, parties, and green tea, taken to the tune of a drunk karaoke soundtrack usually at some cafe. A number of my students were girls this year, so all these things were that much more tricky to pull off. Staying professional meant often doing these things on our students' terms, but they were so shy that we had to provide the topics of conversation with constant flows of questions that felt like quizzes, and that's even if we got an invite. I never invited myself over to someone's home, parties typically needed a reason, and green tea, well,...you only have so many Friday nights. But I also had other audiences than just my students, and those were done in the more accepted local discourse of Vietnamese, and *definitely* on their terms. I drew friendship from three wells, my class, the little street we lived on, and helpers and language learners who had been somehow selected by our culture director Mark over time.

Of these, my two language helpers were the ones I spent the most time with. I have very little memory of the lady teacher except for one tour we took to the local ethnic museum, which I remember only because I have photos. I spent so many hours with a young man named Thai, of whom I have only one photo. We spent them pouring over a movie I was translating called "Chuyen Nha Moc 2," (The Moc Family, Part 2). For part one, I had done my best to just capture the main idea, but this time I was tackling every nuance of the complicated dialog. While I learned a lot of insight, the greatest revelation was that the Vietnamese use more of a code language within the language than I ever imagined in the form of countless proverbs and allusions to ancient stories. This came to me with an overwhelming sense that these references were too complicated for me to risk tossing around. It would be like making a reference to Yoda without knowing he was short, green and good with a lightsaber. My thin veneer of knowledge, however, gave Thai enough material to download naturally without preparing a lesson and we usually combined visits, parties and green tea in one setting.

"Here have some tea, Thai. I'll put on some music and we'll play games. Now...*sigh* the purple book."

The purple book is a thick dictionary of Vietnamese sayings, described only in Vietnamese and I'd been having former teachers highlight the ones they knew (which interestingly was only about 20% of them). I'd been doing these so long that by the time I reached the equivalent of letter 'm' the highlighter on letter 'a' was so faint you couldn't see it any more.

"Here is one I know. "Mỗi thời, mỗi cách." I highlight it.

"So, what does it mean?"

"Um. It's hard to explain. Many timings you can find another way."

"Hm. That's useful. So I will try to use it." And we talk for a few minutes so I can try and use the proverb.

"I know this one. 'Mạnh vì gạo, bạo vì tiền'" So I parrot Thai and ask what this one means.

"It means whatever is the good result, you can do it that way."

"Hmm. That sounds a little dark. We say 'the ends justify the means.'"

"I don't understand that in English," says Thai in Vietnamese. "What do you mean?"

"It is kind of like when students cheat so they get a good result, even though it's wrong."

"Yes,...*that*," mused Thai, nodding.

Others that Thai knew from the thick book, "Mưu sự tại nhân, thành sự tại thiên" We make plans, heaven messes with them or performs them, I couldn't figure which he meant, "Một giọt máu đào hơn ao nước lã." Blood is thicker than water.

"Hey, that sounds kind of familiar. I guess we have something like that."

"Miệng hùm, gan sứa. If you cannot bite, never show your teeth."

"Một nụ cười bằng mười thang thuốc bổ. Laugh and grow fat."

"Tell me more about this one, Thai." I thought of "Laughter is the best medicine."

"It mean that even you have no money, you can be like a millionaire if you can find something funny to laugh about."

"Hmm... I like that one. I've got to find some opportunity to use that. Maybe I'll make one."

There was a single street leading up to the Agricultural University where we lived that had the customary pho (noodle) shop, and a string of tailors, what we called "Wal-marts," and micro-outdoor markets with three or four tables covered in leafy greens. That wasn't a lot to work with, but I managed to make a great friendship with the family that lived right up by the gate that had been primed to some extent by former teachers.

"Hello, I'd like two more sets of clothespins, two of those boxes of matches, a jar of fish sauce and that stapler." This was Wal-Mart. "And I'd like to make twenty copies of this lesson plan."

"So, when are you coming over for dinner again? I'm having soup tonight."

"Oh, really? That's very generous of you. I'll come over tonight and bring you the leftovers we have of banana bread that Katie left me."

We had banana bread coming out of our ears, because the typical thing was to buy or be given a huge clump of bananas and turn the rest into banana bread. I had taught my new teammate Katie how to get the bugs out of the flour with a strand.

"Ok, child. Come tonight. We'll eat when you come and when Thao and Chinh come home. They had two kids about a year apart, like any good family.

"Thank you, ma'am."

"When we were eating, I asked about my students."

"What do students want, do you think?"

They want to save money, was the first obvious answer, to make friends with a foreigner, and to have a special view of the world.

"Do you think they would like American food? I am trying to decide."

"Of course, they love American food."

"What if it is like the food I brought to you last week."

"Oh that? I don't what that was. It is very strange."

I decided to make tacos for the students anyway. I approached the idea of feeding dozens of students from combined classes—Rich and mine—the meal which takes three days to prepare. Pancakes might have been just as well, but I couldn't resist the excited looks in the eyes of Khanh and his parents when I had once had the meal at their home, and the students needed a new practical use for cheese, so I decided to go for it. The three days was no joke. I had a tortilla press that my parents had sent, but it didn't work very well, which was a shame because it had cost a lot send being heavy. After the flour was strained, we tried using it for a while, but ended up rolling them up with a jar instead and cooking them slowly over a light heat. With heaps of shells, we started preparing for the next days' preparation. We chop-chop-chopped for another day until I had a huge vat of diced tomatos, and something that resembled cilantro and, of course, onions. Katie deserves credit for telling me that putting a spoon in your mouth upside down keeps you from crying when you chop an onion. Maybe because it was a popular song at that time, I just barely avoided being stuck with the nickname "spoonman" as we had about thirty onions to chop. The alternative was to make a river of tears like the local legend lady at Coc mountain who lost her lover. My river of tear was simply from being bad with onions.

The third morning was for meat, which Rich and I tackled together and that night, students started pouring in for the grandest party of my career. I still look fondly back on that party as the most well-produced experience, and I longed for the days when we once had the newscasters coming to film our English clubs in Haiphong. Not only had I been working overtime with the food, but I had developed several games which looking back, I could have made money on they were so good. They were all copies of popular American games at the time.

"I made you a whole deck of Taboo." This game is perfect for English learning, except that we did it all entirely in Vietnamese so that they could learn playing it the way we do, in their own language. A problem with simply translating a deck of Taboo cards is that they are so cultural. The following example gives you an idea of what I mean:

They Must Say:	"Independence Day"	"Herbert Hoover"	"Oliver Twist"
They CANT Say:	_alien	_President	_novel
	_spaceship	_White House	_Charles Dickens
	_Will Smith	_depression	_Victoria England
	_movie	_disaster	_poor
	_invasion	_economy	_boy

So, I contextualized the whole thing, so my cards looked like the following:

They Must Say:	"Lotus Flower"	"Ho Chi Minh"	"Bia Hoi"
They CANT Say:	_Buddhist	_President	_drink
	_pond	_beard	_wine
	_bulb	_mausoleum	_yellow
	_flower	_independence	_glass
	_pink	_history	_outing

Words were much simpler, of course, such as teacher, shirt, grasshopper, cyclo, library, bamboo, buffalo, etc. They loved it. In Asia, the thing to do of late has been to copy every single thing in the west that's marketable, but if you can beat 'them' to it, you will be seen as an absolute true genius. However, there were some things I didn't expect. Well. I did. Cheating.

"He said Buddhist. I know he did, I heard it!!"

"I did not."

"He said it in Chinese."

"Oh no. You tell lie." I was about to start a fight with this game.

"Come on, it's just a game. Don't you want to play by the rules to see who is the best one? We'll never know if you find ways to cheat. Besides, there is not any prize.

When we are doing buffalo, someone swore he used a horn sign, but the kid promised he was just swishing his hair.

"Oh no you don't. Who do you think you are?"

"I'm boofalo. Hehe."

"Where have I heard THAT before??"

So, we move onto "Who Wants to Be a Millionaire," when we finished all the cards, and for the sake of telling children and posterity that I did this, I had actually prepared a one million dong prize. I also knew from years of playing Jeopardy that I was quite safe. The Vietnamese can not resist going all or nothing. Ev-er. That's right. I knew 100% that no one was going to walk away with the money before they lost it and I could put it right back into savings. I put up a million dong, or seventy-five dollars as the prize, and we played "Who Wants to Be a Millionaire" with the real amounts.

We had an elimination round, because if we had simply chosen one person, it would not be fun. When we had our three teams narrowed down to three individuals. I used the same rules. If you are not too familiar with the game, the rules say you can call a friend (in our case, ask, because they didn't have phones yet), or you can have two choices taken away. We started with just a hundred dong for an easy multiple-choice question and kept doubling the stakes if they wanted to keep going—all or nothing. Of course, people went through the questions every time until they lost, exactly as I had predicted.

"What does it mean: 'She just got wind of it?' – (A) she ran fast, (B) she understood it, (C) she threw it away, or (D) she had it taken from her." These were the kinds of questions we were asking. Students kept forgetting about their special powers and occasionally, I would remind them.

I almost lost about twenty dollars. One kid had gone far, and he was starting to say "Um. I'll just take the money home." His buddies were all saying, "No, no, you have to play on! Don't be so weak." but he was a smart kid. I had to really bluff.

"That is smart," I said nodding, "If you just take the money, then you'll have enough to buy lunch for everyone. Welllll...*alllll-most* everyone. I think you might need a little more to take the whole class out." I wasn't just arrived to Vietnam yesterday, you know. I knew what kind of pressure he was under if he won.

"You're right. I think I'm going to go juuuuust one more round."

I opened the envelope with a big lump in my throat. If he answers this and walks, I lose forty dollars not twenty. I read.

"The real reason why prices were, and still are, too high is complicated, and no short discussion can satisfactorily explain this problem. What word or phrase best describes prices?" (A) Complicated. (B) Adequately explained. (C) Too high in the past, but now low. (D) Too high in the past and in the present."

"Ha! Got 'em!" He answered "C" and bit the dust.

The whole class was in shock, staring at me incredibly as if I'd just announced the doubling of their school tuition.

That's when I remembered it, like a boss.

"Một nụ cười bằng mười thang thuốc bổ."

"Laugh and grow fat, my friends. Laugh and grow fat."

Back Home

I had forgotten how suspenseful the show 'Wheel of Fortune' was.

"I'd like to buy an 'E.'

Sorry, *beep* ...no 'E,' try again." The lady with the big hair's turn.

Whooosh.

I had been home three days and forgotten a lot of about what living here is like. We were having lasagna tonight, and I didn't know yet why I felt so conflicted inside. After all, I was home—at my parents' home, and I had just moved my body several thousand miles in a couple of days.

"I'd like to solve the puzzle," said big hair. "A long way from Miami." Congratulations, said the host. "Looks like you've won a trip...to China." The woman scowled like she didn't know where China was.

"Dinner's ready, won't you come and find something to drink!" I was home. I was home!

My first memory of this kind of trip home back from Vietnam after my fourth year of teaching, and then an exotic trip to Tibet, followed by color-saturated Summer Teaching program in another part of China, would be in, probably August of 2002. This year was a little bit different, as you know normally I would be teaching again right about now, but I was done for teaching for a while, and looking forward to an extended time off of two or three months. The plan was to hopefully overcome a little bit of mild-burnout with the exotic (if it were even possible that such a thing would be needed) and decompress at home a little, boarding a plane again the following January for Hanoi, where I would study (two chapters ago). After that I went on to teach again (last chapter). My first memory of this trip back home was still in the airport.

This big huge black guy sat down beside me, really friendly, and in my heart I was thinking "whoa, he's so big!!" Another Goliath sat down on the other side of me, and I thought, "whoa, I'm so small!!"

As always, my parents were so happy to see me, and there's always the temptation to try and summarize all year—or even the whole experience—on the first night. Dad wasn't able to come just yet, so I sat with my mom in the car at the Taco Bell drive in.

"Would you like Chalupas, or Djingo Puffs? They are the newest thing. Or the Dorito chips are pretty good, they come in Cool Ranch or the Nacho Cheese kinds, or something called Fresh Daze. Baja blast,...that's new too."

The ordering billboard towered above me.

"Uh, there are cars behind us, and last time I went to Taco Bell it was 'hot, medium or mild?' Maybe we should go inside?"

"Dad will be so happy to see you. Did I tell you he had built a garden fence behind the house?"

I started to realize something; I was selfish to want to be always telling people about the Great Wall.

"No, that's great. How long did it take?"

"A couple days. But we've had some of the first cool weather and it's great to get outside before it gets too cold."

"Has Evan gone back to school yet?" I might have been in trouble for not already knowing that.

"He left a little early to volunteer for something. Lyle's gone too, it's just us this time."

We talked about the Razorbacks, Fall Festivals, and grandmother, who lived at home with us and had come down with dementia and this was consuming much of my mothers' time. It was an increasingly difficult season, but at that point, grandmother could still get out and eat at certain restaurants and do certain things.

   Much of my time that first week was poured into making an exhibit from one of those cardboard displays that are on sale every year in August. Because I took a lot of slide film, I had the extra step of having some of those made into large-sized prints, and then meticulously pasting them onto the boards while agonizing over the short paragraphs of text.

   "Is this too long? Do you think anyone will read this?"

   "It's way too long," said mom, my best editor. "It better be under three sentences."

   "Really?? You don't think anybody will read it?"

   "You haven't been here a while, have you?"

   "Hello ma'am. Yes, nice to... (oh, never mind)."

   I thought she was looking at me, but then I saw a younger girl she was actually coming toward.

   We were in the foyer of the church, and I stood brazenly beside my perfectly cut display board as if I were part of the display.

   "Hello, sir." Somebody finally stopped by.

   "Are you the *missionary*?"

   "Yes, sir. I am." We technically did not identify with that term for all the misunderstanding it could cause, but this is a church and we are talking about travel.

   "Well that's great. My niece went to China." My board didn't say anything about China.

   "Well, that's wonderful. How old is your niece?"

"Oh, she's eighteen. She went with her church."

"Is that so? Not this church?"

"No, she lives in Texas. Well, now. This is just great. You go and be safe over there, ok?"

"Wait, don't you want to—" He already moved on, I was going to say "hear about Vietnam?"

The church was having a world awareness seminar, something like that, but only two or three other people came by the display. Nobody read it. I was invisible, but thankfully, in this instance, I had a chance to force myself on people from the pulpit, which is becoming an increasingly rare opportunity. I said who I was and what I had done. The previous time I had five minutes, but this time was almost like a parade where you just walk by and wave, but still, I kept a mantra up and going, "Just let them see your face and your name. Let them put your face with your name. That's all."

The worship music was intense, lasting almost half an hour, and the sermon about having conviction and being a good neighbor.

You wanna go try that new Vietnamese restaurant today? I think my family could tell I was a little deflated after the church service and all that work on the board.

"Nobody even looked at it, after all we put in to it," I moaned.

"Well, ...*I know*. There'll be other chances to use it."

That's right! There was a new Vietnamese restaurant, actually two that had come to Little Rock. Vietnamese food was indeed the new discovery and I was surprised to not find people at least asking about that. It turns out; a lot of Vietnamese in Arkansas had been hiding under a 'Chinese' name in their businesses until recently, when it started feeling safer to be themselves. The times were a' changin'. When the new Vietnamese establishment had shown itself to be successful, another one opened up on Cantrell.

We were greeted, and I was anxious to say something in Vietnamese, since it had been already almost ten days here.

"Anh co noi tieng Viet duoc khong?" I blurted out.

She looked at me funny and made a motion like "one moment, please." A young man came to our table and answered the question, when I repeated it.

"Co, anh noi Tieng Viet, ha anh?" His Vietnamese sounded like that Southern-style Vietnamese nasal voice I had once heard on the language tapes before leaving. My northern brand of speech was probably a little strange here, but even the attempt must have been appreciated.

As I looked around me, the children were all starting to stare. They were mesmerized. Several waiters surrounded me and daintily laid napkins in front of me, setting up the silverware. Another Vietnamese man hopped up from his table and walked boldly up to me, pointing to his camera, hoping that he and I could have a picture together. "Excuse me," he said.

"Excuse me,"

"Snap out of it, Hayden. He's wondering what you want to order." I suddenly came to. I was sitting in the restaurant in America. Nobody was watching me, and certainly nobody wanted my picture.

"Oh yes, um...pho maybe?"

"Ok, beef, chicken, pork, buff, or veg?"

"Um...chick—en?"

"Would you like salt, cinnamon, or soy on it?"

"Um. I don't know! We never had to choose these things in Vietnam. Just pho! Which always had MSG. But I would like chopsticks." There weren't any on the table.

"Yes, sir. Coming up." We all had the same thing, but he brought me some chopsticks.

"Now, you'll have to tell us how to eat it," said mom.

"You know. You've been to Vietnam."

"Ha ha, that's just what everyone says. Oh, look he's bringing us tea, just like the old days."

When we got the bill, I was shocked though. "Three dollars *each*, for *green tea*??? What? It's free in Vietnam!"

"Well, it's too late now, to good health!"

"Good health and flat wallets."

We drove around town and looked at all the new stuff.

"Look over there, 'Ross Dress For Less.' That's new. 'And did you know we are getting a new 'Chick-fil-a?"

"Is that so?"

"And see that over there?"

"Hm, it's Kroger," I said.

"Yes, but *can't you tell*? They are getting a makeover. Say, let's all go in the new Ross and get you some new pants, I can see you've got streaks all over those."

We did that, and mom was getting some new things too. "They don't gush all over your height and bust size here," I said. We all thought that was funny, as mom must have understood from her visit two years before.

Dad also wanted to go into Home Depot and buy some boards. "I think we'll have to go home and grab the other car though. There's no way they'll ever fit in this one."

"Oh come on, dad. How big can they be? I bet we could just strap 'em on."

"Hayden, you're not in Vietnam any more, son."

"Oh, yeah. Right."

When we are in Home Depot, dad and I, we meet a friend.

"Why hello there! Whose *this* guy? Back from the orient, I see."

"Yes," I smiled timidly. "I've been in Vietnam."

"You know, I was in Vietnam once."

"No," I perked up, "I didn't know that! Was probably not like it is now." I wasn't sure quite where this was going to go.

"No, but I was only there two years, and I mostly did engineering." I felt relief if he talked about it that way.

"Well, you should come by sometime. I've got lots of pictures. I'd like to see yours."

"So, just tell me. How was your trip? By the way, did you know Jenny's pregnant?" he turned to dad.

"I wasn't sure if I was supposed to tell him now, or…"

Never mind his phone rang. Dad and I sat waiting a couple minutes, while I looked at 'eye-rings' in the display board. "Everything is so organized here, can you believe it, dad?"

"Hey listen, I'll have to take a rain check. You be safe over there in China, now, y'hear?"

"Sure!" I said. I realized I still didn't have that zinger of a two-sentence summary in my mind yet, anyway.

Especially for China.

Did you like these stories?

See what Vietnam looks like

and explore more stories at

www.haydensvietnambook.com

Standing At The Edge of Tomorrow

(A Complete Memoir of the Years in Vietnam, 1998-2004, unpublished)

Readers of this first edition who also give to my newest campaign will be able to access the full archives of material in a larger collection. For more information on how you can add value to this effort to bring joy to the developing world, contact me on my website: haydensvietnambook.com and tell me a little about yourself.

You can also enjoy access to the following set of essays:

Chapter 1: That Day I had One Heck of an Idea

Chapter 2: Landing Day

Chapter 3: Still Alive On Highway Five

Chapter 4: Khoa and the Yellow Traffic Light

Chapter 5: My First Day As a Teacher

Chapter 6: The First Day I was Late, the Second Day I Left Early, the Third Day I Didn't Go At All

Chapter 7: Halong Bay Back Then

Chapter 8: No Place Like Que

Chapter 9: Girls Just Wanna Have Fun

Chapter 10: The Fish and the Cross Mean Something Different Here

Chapter 11: Day In, Day Out

Chapter 12: Manchester Madness

Chapter 13: Little Blue Tables

Chapter 14: On Language: "Em Đi Đâu Đay?"

Chapter 15: Skin and Brawn

Chapter 16: The Great Aperture

Chapter 17: Cat Ba Daze: CBD's for BVD's

Chapter 18: Home Away From Home

Chapter 19: What Doesn't Fail You Makes You Smarter

Chapter 20: Year-end Reflections

Chapter 21: Ghosthunting

Chapter 22: Tunnel Rat

Chapter 23: Field of Nightmares

Chapter 24: Summer of '68

Chapter 25: Ho Chi Minh

Chapter 26: The Hilton in Hanoi

Chapter 27: Laos Warming Party

Chapter 28: The War on Film

Chapter 29: Teacher, We're Camping!

Chapter 30: The Christian Patriot

Chapter 31: Landing in the New Normal

Chapter 32: Calling Class 911

Chapter 33: "Mandarin Mark" and VHVY

Chapter 34: Mom and Dad's Visit

Chapter 35: Hip Hip Halong

Chapter 36: Manny and Me

Chapter 37: Captain Go's Beauty Show

Chapter 38: Fifteen Minutes of Fame

Chapter 39: A Dream in Hanoi

Chapter 40: The Lancing Queen

Chapter 41: Cao Bang Bling

Chapter 42: The Road to Fluevia

Chapter 43: Cát Bà on a Shoestring

Chapter 44: Professor Stellar

Chapter 45: Hmong Friends

Chapter 46: Oh Brother, Where Art Thou?

Chapter 47: Return Journeys to Four Cities

Chapter 48: Three Amigos Become Dalat Cowboys

Chapter 49: Things We Learned On the Road

Chapter 50: Field Notes on Loneliness, Faith and Death

Chapter 51: Party Like It's 1999

Chapter 52: Before and After

Chapter 53: September Twelfth

Chapter 54: Paint My Love

Chapter 55: Toshiba, Inc.

Chapter 56: Blue Suede Shoes

Chapter 57: The Promised Festival

Chapter 58: Total Vietnamese Friendships

Chapter 59: Two Ambassadors

Chapter 60: Leaving Behind a Changing Landscape

Chapter 61: Evangetinkering

Chapter 62: Captain Solo

Chapter 63: The Mango Banana Pancakes Club

Chapter 64: People Who Shook History

Chapter 65: Jingle (Mission) Bells

Chapter 66: A Friend in the Faith

Chapter 67: The Challenge of Vietnamese Culture

Chapter 68: We Tried Everything

Chapter 69: Simply The Story

Chapter 70: Three-Self Conversation

Chapter 71: The Place and Day I First Became a Poet

Chapter 72: A Walk Around Hoan Kiem Lake

Chapter 74: The Bird Releasing Festival

Chapter 73: The Language Centre

Chapter 75: Chuyen Nha Moc

Chapter 76: Bombs in Iraq

Chapter 77: Expats

Chapter 78: Perfume Passion

Chapter 79: Documenteering

Chapter 80: Party Like It's 1000 (Seven Years Later)

Chapter 81: The Final Year

Chapter 82: Bamboo Grove

Chapter 83: Accident Prone

Chapter 84: What About a Picnic?

Chapter 85: Sasse Swan Song

Chapter 86: Tet, the Vietnamese New Year

Chapter 87: We Are Millionaires Already

Chapter 88: Adventures With Diane

Chapter 89: The Lost Guitar

Chapter 90: Sharing With The Vietnamese

Chapter 91: Back Home

Chapter 92: Ruth and Manny

Chapter 93: A View From Next Door

Chapter 94: Tet, Redux

Chapter 95: Frank and Tina

Chapter 96: We are Adults Now, Aren't We?

Chapter 97: Merry, Marry.

Chapter 98: A Visit to America

Chapter 99: The Buffalo Hustler

Chapter 100: You Never Really Leave

CPSIA information can be obtained
at www.ICGtesting.com
Printed in the USA
BVHW01s0824150818
524584BV00009B/87/P

9 780998 432304